THE Male-Female CHURCH STAFF

*Celebrating
The Gifts*

◆

*Confronting
The Challenges*

◆

Anne Marie Nuechterlein
Celia Allison Hahn

AN ALBAN INSTITUTE PUBLICATION

The Publications Program of The Alban Institute is assisted by a grant from Trinity Church, New York City.

Library of Congress Catalog Card #90-83134
ISBN 1-56699-038-6

CONTENTS

89795

The situation of clergy and lay professionals in multiple staff teams has been inadequately explored by researchers and theorists concerned with church leadership. I can count on one hand the useful books I know on multiple staff ministries, and still have fingers left over!

This book is greatly needed. It is in multiple staff teams that clergy must learn to collaborate and negotiate with people every day (not just a few nights a month at board and committee meetings); it is in multiple staff teams that clergy explore and live out their commitments to just and appropriate relationships between men and women in working teams; it is in multiple staff teams that clergy explore and deal with the tensions created between the needs to function as specialists and as generalists.

This book not only addresses these issues, but it also moves us substantially toward understanding them and gives advice for dealing with them. The reader will find here practical and interesting reflections on structure and power, communication, gender, and sexuality in teams.

The book was long in the making. One of the characteristics of a collaborative process is that it takes time. Hahn and Nuechterlein collaborated not only with one another, but also with the others they invited to join them in editing, critiquing, and suggesting.

The journey was not easy. However, it has produced a fine piece of work that explicates the proposed theories and practice.

The authors bring their own unique thinking to these subjects. You will not find here the commonplace or warmed-over canards, but the insightful reflections of two professionals who have done their homework in the literature, lived the experience of female-male teams in their own work settings, distilled the experience of practitioners, and brought their own original and profound thinking to the topic. Read on and enjoy.

Speed B. Leas
Director of Consultation
The Alban Institute

More and more churches are discovering the new opportunities—
and the new kinds of stresses—that come when men and women
work together as colleagues in ministry on church staffs.

There are gifts to celebrate. Such churches and their staff teams
know a new richness in their ministry. More differences lead to
more stretching, more excitement, and growth. A broader range of
strengths in the church leadership enhances ministry with the
whole people of God.

And there are challenges to confront. The staff members may
encounter some puzzlement, disagreement, and conflict about basic
assumptions as they learn to minister in concert.

We believed it would be helpful to write a book that encourages
male-female staff teams to celebrate the richness of differences and
to explore the mixture of assumptions, styles, and postures they
bring together in their work. Through such celebration and
exploration such teams could see their differences as benefits, not
barriers, to their relationship and work as colleagues.

This book is written primarily for female-male teams of ordained
or lay professionals who work on the staff of a local church. We
hope that it will also be useful for churches considering a male-
female team, for solo pastors who want to enhance their
partnership in ministry with lay leaders, for pastors and seminary
students who work together in internship or fieldwork
arrangements, and for judicatory and seminary personnel who want
to facilitate growth in ministry for pastors and students.

We recommend that men and women working together in any
of these settings use this book collaboratively for reading and discussion. You might take a chapter each week, reading it individually
and reflecting on your own experience with the help of the
questions at the end of the chapter, then adding a half-hour to an

hour to the weekly staff meeting to discuss the issues from the chapter that seem most relevant to your staff team. The questions are written for two colleagues; rephrase as appropriate if your staff team is larger.

Every human encounter and event is complex. Although we are focusing on the male-female dimension of church staff teams in this book, we need to recognize that many dimensions shape the interaction of men and women as they work together—age, tenure, status, formal roles, skills, race and ethnic background, birth order, temperament, and more.

A further layer of complexity arises because there are no clear ways of describing how men act and how women act. The best we can do is to hint at and describe tendencies toward differences. You will find points at which you identify with tendencies ascribed to someone of the other sex. To make matters more complicated, at this period in the church's life we can observe many male leaders who have strongly developed "feminine" strengths, and many clergywomen who have had to develop "masculine" strengths in order to break into a profession previously closed to women. Thus, generalizations that one might make about men and women in the general culture become less applicable when used to describe the church staff team.

Yet, in spite of all these complexities that make a clear picture impossible, most of us conclude that men and women are not the same. We live in, and from, bodies that have significant differences. We are like, or unlike, the parent who probably provided us with our first and most formative care. So, urging that you plant all these caveats firmly in your mind, we will proceed to describe some of the dynamics, dilemmas, and delights we have seen women and men encounter on the church staff.

A Note About the Myers-Briggs Type Indicator

Many church staff members have discovered that the Myers-Briggs Type Indicator (MBTI) provides insights into their own strengths, appreciation for the different gifts of others, and a language for talking about differences with colleagues. If you are not familiar with this helpful tool for understanding human differences, a brief introduction may lay the groundwork for occasional references to the MBTI in the text.

When you take this forced-choice test, you will find that your expressed preferences place you in one of sixteen four-letter types. Let's explore the meaning of the *second* letter first. We all take in information. Some of us prefer to stick with the facts, the data we can see and touch and hear and smell: Sensing is our preferred way of taking in information. We are practical, down-to-earth, patient with financial details and tasks related to building maintenance. Others of us prefer to take in information through intuition. Meanings and metaphors are our stock in trade: the facts always point beyond themselves. Symbols are highly significant to us, and we get excited when we dream about how the future of our church might unfold. Our preference for taking in information by Sensing or iNtuiting is signaled by an S or an N in our MBTI type.

We all make decisions. Some of us prefer to be led in our deciding by our heads: we figure out what the logical consequences of a proposed action are likely to be and determine which choice *objectively* makes best sense; those of us with this Thinking preference choose that option. Others of us are more likely to be led by our hearts: we make our decisions on the basis of *who* and *what* is important to us. Our values and relationships lead those of us with this Feeling preference toward more *subjective* grounds for decision making. The third letter of our MBTI type is a *T* for Thinking or an *F* for Feeling. Here is the one preference in which men and women tend to show some consistent differences. In the general population, more men prefer Thinking and more women prefer Feeling. In the clergy population, a higher percentage of men with a Feeling preference blurs this distinction.

The terms *Extraversion* and *Introversion* have found their way into our daily speech. Those of us who are Extraverts are energized by being with people. We feel more alive in a large group, and we can even think better by talking things out with friends. The Introvert is energized by quiet times of thinking or meditation; thus replenished, the Introvert can venture forth to the world of human encounters again. Those of us who are Introverts will be helped by a chance to look over the agenda in advance of the meeting, and we may not be clear about our own reaction to the meeting until we have had a chance to reflect on it later in solitude. And so an *I* or an *E* introduces the four-letter type.

The last letter, *J* or *P*, indicates whether we would prefer to live our lives in a planned, orderly way, making lists and checking the tasks off one by one (Judging); or respond to life as it comes, staying flexible and rolling with the punches (Perceiving).

David Keirsey has noticed that the sixteen possible combinations of these four letters can be grouped under four temperaments, each indicated by two of the four letters. The person with an iNtuitive Feeling (NF) temperament is a catalyst, a self-actualizer deeply involved in helping people grow. The iNtuitive Thinker (NT) is a visionary, an idea person who seeks to become more and more competent. The SJ (Sensing Judging) is a traditionalist, a stablizer who dutifully performs the tasks that help an organization run more smoothly. The SP (Sensing Perceiving) loves action, shines as a troubleshooter or crisis counselor, and prizes freedom and flexibility.[1]

Members of staff teams benefit most from their understanding of type and temperament when they use it not to justify their behavior, but to celebrate their own and others' gifts, to work with differences on the staff, and to learn over the years how their least developed functions can be used in a positive way.

Acknowledgements

We want to express our thanks to those who read the first manuscript of this book and made helpful criticisms. The senior staff of The Alban Institute provided helpful feedback (Loren Mead, Leslie Buhler, Speed Leas, Roy Oswald, Caroline Hughes, George Parsons, Margaret Bruehl, Roy Pneuman, Bob McLaughlin, Marie Schumann, and Linda Ewald.) Pamela Read and Rhonda Hanisch read the manuscript several times and offered excellent criticisms. Speed Leas was responsive above and beyond the call of duty and provided some much needed correctives to the perspectives of two female writers. We are also grateful for insightful comments from Edward A. White, Alban Institute consultant; William Adix, chaplain at Emanuel Hospital in Portland, Oregon; Durwood ("Bud") Buchheim, professor of preaching at Wartburg Theological Seminary, Dubuque, Iowa; Susan Blackburn Heath, canon theologian at Trinity Cathedral, Columbia, South Carolina; Barbara Gilbert, pastoral counselor and author in Jaffrey Center, New Hampshire; and Fran Odden, pastor at Bay Shore Lutheran Church, Milwaukee, Wisconsin. In addition, Caroline Engelbrecht, Wartburg Theological Seminary; Harold Eppley, parish pastor at Regent Congregational/Lutheran Church, Regent, North Dakota; and Jim Melvin, newly ordained parish pastor, gave valued assistance to this project.

We appreciate the useful critical comments of staff teams: Bob Trache and Betty Wanamaker at Immanuel-Church-on-the-Hill in Alexandria, Virginia; Judith McCall and Gilbert Splett at St. John Lutheran Church, Madison, Wisconsin; and Dennis Dickman, Evon Flesberg, and Glen Wheeler at St. Paul Lutheran Church in Waverly, Iowa.

We are grateful for the comments of our critical readers. The final responsibility for this book is ours.

Celia Allison Hahn

Anne Marie Nuechterlein

NOTE

1. David Keirsey, Marilyn Bates, *Please Understand Me* (Del Mar, CA: Prometheus Nemesis Book Company, 1987). See also Roy M. Oswald and Otto Kroeger, *Personality Type and Religious Leadership* (Washington, DC: The Alban Institute, 1988).

CHAPTER I

Who Are We as Women and Men?

Susan Berger, associate pastor at St. Mark's, approached this Monday's meeting with Charles Williams, the senior pastor, with some apprehension. They had always met weekly for general planning and scheduling. But today Susan had another agenda. Although Susan and Charles have never been close personal friends, their working relationship has been cordial and effective. In the past month, however, Susan had been wondering why Charles seemed aloof. Why did his mind always seem miles away?

Susan knocked tentatively on Charles's office door, moved to the chair next to his desk, took a deep breath, and plunged in. "Charles, lately I've had the feeling your mind seems to be somewhere else. Is there something wrong? Anything I need to know about?"

Charles sat in silence wondering whether to tell her what he was struggling with. What would she think? Finally he began speaking in a matter-of-fact tone of voice: "An old friend from grade school died four weeks ago."

Susan said quietly, "I'm sorry." Leaning forward a bit, she asked, "Were you close?"

"Yes," said Charles, clearing his throat.

As the silence stretched out awkwardly, Charles found himself ill-at-ease under Susan's searching gaze as she sat across from him, apparently deep in thought. Loosening his tie, Charles stood up, began pacing around his office, and spoke in an agitated and halting voice. "Earl died of a heart attack. He was the kind of guy who cared about things a lot—maybe too much. But I liked him."

Susan leaned forward. "And he cared about you."

"Yes," said Charles, slowly sitting down.

As Susan and Charles have discovered, many staff relationships move along a smooth path until staff members find themselves emotionally vulnerable. When deep feelings arise, our male-female differences may become more evident and more likely to create discomfort within the relationship. The discomfort often presses us toward questions we struggle to articulate: Who am I as a woman or a man? How am I going to relate to this person as my colleague? Our answers to these questions will shape our ministry.

Most men and women in ministry evidence both "feminine" and "masculine" characteristics. On church staffs we may discover women who exercise more masculine strengths and men whose gifts seem more typically feminine. Yet we can discern general tendencies toward differences between women and men. In this book we will be exploring how we as men and women in ministry are affected by our own genders, by each other's genders, and by attitudes about gender held by members of our congregation and even by the culture in which we live. Gender differences are interwoven with many other threads that form the tapestry of our lives and relationships. We will become more effective colleagues in ministry as we become more fully aware of who we are—physically, sexually, emotionally, spiritually, intellectually, and relationally.

As you pursue the following questions, ponder their shape in your own life, and imagine what shape they might take in the life of your colleague. Then take time to exchange viewpoints and learn from one another.

Who Am I Physically?

What do our bodies—the way we experience them, move them, communicate through them—have to do with our ministry? Our attitudes toward our body-selves have been shaped by all sorts of messages from our culture and our religious tradition. How do those attitudes find expression in our roles as people in ministry?

When he was still a small boy, the culture gave Charles clear messages about what it meant to be male, what it meant to live in and through a male body. He learned that his teachers, parents, and peers respected him more when he ran fast, played hard, and never gave up the fight. He also noticed that people responded less positively to Earl, with his emotional response to people and disinterest in games. Charles was pained when he saw his friend rejected by his peers for he really liked Earl's sensitivity and warmth. Although Charles wanted to be like Earl, he wanted even more to be admired by his parents and teachers and friends. So Charles downplayed the emotional and expressive dimension of who he was. When Earl died, Charles wondered if something had died within himself.

In pastoral ministry, Charles has learned to express his authority through his six-foot-tall body. His big frame is part of who he is as a teacher and preacher. In the pulpit his strong, expansive gestures accompany his words about God's power, judgment, and steadfast love. He paces energetically around the classroom. Charles holds a patient's hand in the hospital or shakes hands after church with a strong grip.

Susan also received some early messages. She felt approved of, somehow "right," when she played quietly with her dolls and moved gracefully to and fro on the swing. She learned to convey gentleness and sensitivity through body language. She instinctively leans closer to Charles as she senses his pain. Her expressions are mobile and responsive. Her concern in a counseling session, her joy in hymn singing are easy for parishioners to read. In her preaching she sometimes uses small, round gestures as she speaks of God's tender compassion. Her quiet listening and gentle touch convey responsiveness and empathy.

Of course Charles can make gentle gestures, and Susan can speak forcefully. Charles will find his ministry strengthened as he embraces the Earl in his own heart; Susan finds her growing edge in standing firm, assertively raising uncomfortable questions about her working relationship with Charles even when she finds it difficult to do so. "Embracing" and "standing firm," when put together, represent wholeness in ministry.

Who Am I Sexually?

An important component of who we are physically is our sexuality. What does it mean to be a sexual being? How does our sexuality as women and men affect our staff relationships?

Because we, as men and women, are sexual beings, all our relationships participate in our sexuality to some degree. Whether we are working with people of the same or the other sex, our sexuality forms one dimension of our working relationship. Even though God created us to be sexual creatures and pronounced our sexuality "very good," many of us find it difficult to think or talk about ourselves as sexual people and to affirm our sexuality as a healthy component of who we are.[1] The sexuality we find so awkward to own is frequently a hidden cause of conflict in our relationships.

Susan and Charles seem to be reasonably comfortable in using their female and male bodies to communicate. Yet some of us find ourselves uncomfortable with our physical selves and with our maleness or femaleness. We have bought into the myth that ministers are sexless.

When we are uncomfortable with our sexuality, we may try to avoid it by behaving and dressing in ways that are asexual. We may also avoid recognizing the sexuality of our colleagues by thinking of them as mothers or fathers, sons or daughters, rather than as women or men. Because our sexuality can be the occasion for pain and difficulty in our staff relationships, we need to work at becoming more aware of who we are as sexual beings and how we interact as sexual beings with one another.

Who Am I Emotionally?

How does who we are emotionally influence us as men and women in ministry? Those early messages from the culture often make it harder for men to express their emotions. Charles has deep feelings, but because he was raised to believe that emotional expressiveness was a sign of weakness, he struggles to decide whether and how to express his feelings. Despite his strong feelings Charles communicates emotional distance to Susan, though that is not the message he wants to send her. The constricted emotional style of many male pastors often results in mixed signals and misunderstandings, causing discomfort for them and their colleagues in ministry.

Women, on the other hand, have been culturally conditioned to express their emotions. Susan, for example, often believes that her behavior is ruled by her emotions. She discounts her ability to mobilize her thinking function and bring it to bear on her feelings. Although she finds it natural to raise emotional issues with her col-league, she has come to feel some anxiety about such impulses. Standing ready to knock at Charles's door, Susan worried, Is this okay to do? Am I being an emotional woman? She has noticed that a lot of church leaders skip over the emotional issues in meetings so that they can get on with the agenda and get more work done. Yet she remains convinced that sitting on feelings inhibits communication and team building and reduces trust.

Charles wants to learn how to express his emotions more easily, and Susan wants to become more confident of her ability to integrate thinking and feeling. When we, like Susan and Charles, expand our freedom and capacity to make choices in the emotional dimension of our lives, we grow as individuals, as colleagues, and as ministers.

Keep in mind, however, that we do ourselves and each other an injustice when we assume that women are more emotional and that men are less emotional. It is important that we take the time to get to know this colleague, to hear what this person is saying. Sometimes we get into difficulties in our staff relationships when we assume that our colleagues feel or do not feel a certain way.

Who Am I Spiritually?

How does who we are spiritually as women and men in Christ influence our staff relationships in ministry? How do our spiritual differences affect our staff relationships?

One study of clergy couples (two pastors married to one another) found that men and women had quite different ways of seeking spiritual nourishment. It was the women who said they thought of friendships as integral to their spiritual lives or who reported relational disciplines like praying as couples or families.[2] Historically, more detached and solitary spiritual paths have been typical for men.

Susan and Charles have different spiritualities, different views of God, and different preferences for the language and images they use in describing God. Susan finds the word spirituality helpful in expressing her personal relationship with God. When asked about her spirituality, she describes how God comes to her in worship, in close relationships with other people, in meditation, in prayer, and in keeping a journal. Charles finds it more difficult to speak to others of his deep relationship with God.

Charles and Susan also have different views of God. Charles has been sympathetic with feminists on most issues, and it is becoming more and more natural for him to use inclusive language for God. Charles's strong attachment to the image of God as Father is reflected in his prayers and preaching; nevertheless, out of an awakening sense that there might be some promise for him in different perceptions of God, he recently signed up for a retreat that included meditations on feminine images of God.

Susan frequently uses female imagery and language for God in her sermons and her everyday speech. Though some members of the congregation have objected to her inclusive language, Susan has been pleased that a number of women and men have openly expressed their appreciation to her for helping them open up new dimensions of their faith. Women often tell her that her sermon examples provide them with concrete and accessible ways to connect with God.

Such diversity in imagery of God can enrich the spiritual repertoire not only of the staff but also of the congregation. The woman who has been sexually abused by her father has trouble with Father imagery and is helped by Susan's image of a nurturing Mother God. The aging man or woman in the final stages of life who has lived in the context of a positive and supportive patriarchal family structure is comforted and sustained by the familiar thought of a heavenly Father in Charles's preaching and prayers. When male and female leaders join their imagery they can help bring these parishioners together into a community of faith that does not limit its God by exclusive gender identifications.

Who Am I Intellectually?

How does our intellectual makeup as women and men influence our staff relationships? The intellectual life of ministers—ordained or lay professionals—is a significant dimension of the way we function and the way we are seen by parishioners.

We may have unexamined beliefs about how men think and how women think. Though women enter college with higher records of achievement overall, the low number of women receiving doctoral degrees may give credence to an assumption that women are somehow less intellectually competent than men. If men are seen as intellectually superior, intellectual tasks such as biblical research may be unthinkingly assigned to the male pastor. Susan, as a female pastor, may have to assert her theological competence. Staffs will need to take explicit steps to ensure that intellectual tasks are assigned on the basis of criteria other than gender.

There are indications, however, that men and women may tend to approach intellectual work differently. In *The Behavioral and Brain Sciences,* Jeanette McGlone argues that the brain's hemispheres are more separated in men, more integrated in women.[3] V. Mary Stewart reports that men tend to be more analytic or field independent so that things are "perceived as discrete and separate from the context (perceptual, intellectual, social, or emo-tional) in which they appear."[4] Women tend to be more global or field dependent, which means that they are more likely to see things as part of a whole. These different characteristics seem to reflect a general wish on the part of women to seek integration, to emphasize the connection between people and ideas; and a tendency on the part of men to analyze, discriminate, and notice distinctions.

Some of these differences are reflected in the ways women and men preach. In Susan's preaching, for example, parishioners have noticed her way of interweaving her own life experiences with biblical and theological points. Parishioners note that Charles does not talk about his own life experiences. Instead, he tells stories about other people to illustrate his main points, which are developed through a crystal-clear linear structure.

Female-male pastoral teams gain a sense of the richness of their ministry by becoming aware of their different styles of learning, teaching, and preaching. Examining the many ways we learn, think, and express ourselves enhances our ability to use our intellectual gifts in staff planning and parish ministry.

Who Am I as a Self in Relationships with Others?

All of us as human beings may sometimes find ourselves caught between two basic needs: the need to define ourselves clearly as an "I," to be free, to stake out our personal boundaries; and the need to be close, to be part of a "we," to live in commitment with others.

Men initially seek their identity as males by distinguishing themselves from their female parent. As a result, men tend to value freedom and self-differentiation throughout their lives and will need to have their maleness clearly established before they can reach out and reconnect with women. Men often identify themselves by telling what distinguishes them from others—referring to their roles as senior pastor or committee chairman, or mentioning specific achievements.

Women have a different way of arriving at their sense of themselves. Because a growing girl finds her identity as female naturally unfolding alongside her intimate connection with a parent who is a woman, just as she will someday be, she does not have the same need to pull away and strike out on her own in order to claim her feminine identity. In contrast to her male colleague, she often tells who she is by telling about her connections with others—that she is a member of her women's group, a mother, a daughter, a wife. While male church leaders may tend to define themselves by their work and their achievements, female church leaders may tend to center their sense of self in staff relationships and in the network of parish relationships.

As a woman, Susan may find the nurturing side of her personality dominant in pastoral settings; as a male, Charles's leadership may tend to take on a more directive nature. Or, as a woman, Susan may be *expected* to be more nurturing, and if she fails to meet those expectations, people may become angry with her and think of her as "cold, hard, and uncaring." As a man, Charles may be *expected* to be more directive, and if he is not, people may become angry with him and think of him as "soft, weak, and ineffective." In the interplay between congregational expectations and the real nature of their own pastoral strengths, Charles and Susan may find the possibility for conflict or the opportunity to expand their pastoral effectiveness.

Charles and Susan may also notice that their tendencies toward connection or separation may lead them to different kinds of moral judgments. The feminine ethic is more often derived from relationships than from principles. Though this ethic of relatedness ranks lower on hierarchies of moral development designed by men,[5] church staffs may find it makes an equally important contribution to resolving the ethical dilemmas that emerge in everyday parish life. When Susan and Charles struggled through a church conflict about race relations and response to apartheid, they brought a broader range of viewpoints to this challenge. He contributed his clarity about moral principles and commitment to fairness, and she her sensitivity to the effect of the conflict on the congregation and the neighborhood.

A tendency toward connection or separation may also be an important dimension of how Charles's and Susan's spouses relate to the church and its ordained leaders, and how the spouses are perceived by others. Women married to clergy have traditionally been encouraged to see themselves as partners to the pastor, for example, leading prayers for the women's group and playing the organ on Sundays. Although there have been positive aspects to this sense of partnership, such clergy wives can also get enmeshed in baffling and destructive triangled relationships with their husbands and parishioners.* For example, parishioners may avoid the anxiety-producing prospect of criticizing the pastor by passing the criticism through the pastor's wife. She needs to avoid being triangulated by encouraging parishioners to go directly to the pastor.[6] In contrast, a

---

*Triangling involves any three persons, things, or issues. An emotional triangle is formed when two parts of a system are uncomfortable with the third part of the system. The two parts "triangle in" the third person or issue in order to balance their relationship with one another and to relieve their discomfort. A family triangle might be composed of mother, father, and child. Parish triangles might include the senior pastor, associate pastor, and the senior pastor's spouse; or the senior pastor, the director of Christian education, and the secretary.

husband of a pastor has a clear sense of his own separate identity, and can be supportive of his wife's ministry without getting triangled between pastor and parish.[7]

Many of the factors that influence male-female staff relationships are related to gender. Reflecting upon who we are physically, sexually, emotionally, spiritually, intellectually, and relationally will yield helpful insights into ourselves, our work with one another, and our ministry in the parish. AMN

Questions for Reflection and Discussion

As you reflect on what you bring to your partnership out of your own physical, sexual, emotional, spiritual, intellectual, and relational self, ask yourself:

1. *What are three gifts I bring that are important to the congregation?*
2. *What are three gifts I appreciate in my colleague?*
3. *What is an area of potential or actual conflict?*
4. *Where do our gifts complement each other?*
5. *What do I appreciate most about my colleague's way of relating to me and working with me?*
6. *What do I need most from my colleague to enhance our partnership on the church staff?*

Bring your answers to these questions to your staff meeting, and compare notes with your colleague.

NOTES

1. Anne Marie Nuechterlein, *Improving Your Multiple Staff Ministry* (Minneapolis: Augsburg, 1989), 110.

2. Roy M. Oswald, Michael Tamorria, and Dana V. E. Tamorria (unpublished research on clergy couples, The Alban Institute, Washington, DC).

3. Jeanette McGlone, *The Behavioral and Brain Sciences* cited by Rosemary Radford Ruether in *Sexism and God Talk* (Boston: Beacon Press, 1983), 112.

4. V. Mary Stewart, "Cognitive Style, North American Values, and the Body of Christ," *Journal of Psychology and Theology* 2 (1974): 82.

5. Carol Gilligan, *In a Different Voice* (Cambridge: Harvard University Press, 1982).

6. For helpful discussions of these dynamics, see Lyndon Whybrew, *Minister, Wife, and Church: Unlocking the Triangles* (Washington, DC: The Alban Institute, 1984); and Edwin H. Friedman, *Generation to Generation* (New York: Guilford Press, 1985).

7. Laura Deming and Jack Stubbs, *Men Married to Ministers* (Washington, DC: The Alban Institute, 1986).

CHAPTER II

Self-Esteem

Pastor Larry Edwards and Associate Pastor Barbara Jennings are ministers at St. Matthew's United Methodist Church. Larry, age forty, has been in ordained parish ministry for fourteen years. He is bright and creative and has a strong interest in worship and liturgy. A sensitive, compassionate man whose highest priority is being available for people, he is relaxed, easygoing, quiet, and a good listener. Members of the parish and community find him a caring and gentle person who is helpful when they are struggling, and a congenial and fun-loving person in social situations. At the same time, though, members of the parish and staff struggle with Larry's inability to be decisive about important issues. When it comes to decision making, Larry procrastinates. He feels affirmed by his parishioners, but despite their praise, he wonders whether he is indeed a worthwhile person and an able professional.

Barbara, age forty-five, has been in ordained parish ministry for eleven years. Before going to seminary, she worked as a youth and education director at a church for nine years. Barbara is a caring, perceptive person who responds with warmth, vulnerability, and openness to people in need. Her whole life is centered on the church. She is often asked to be on committees and task forces of the denomination. Members of the parish and community perceive her to be strong, competent, and emotionally expressive. She is willing to ask hard questions of herself, of Larry, and of others. Yet, she often wonders whether what she has to say in meetings is worthwhile. She is unsure of herself and has often felt that she has been successful in spite of herself. While she believes that her ministry is important, she also wonders at times whether she indeed has something to offer the people at her parish.

The Myers-Briggs Type Indicator (MBTI) shows that the two pastors have much in common. Larry is an ENTP and Barbara is an

ENFJ, which means that they both are more energized by people (Extroverted) rather than ideas (Introverted), and they both tend to be more creative (iNtuitive) than practical and detail-oriented (Sensing). As a J (Judging), Barbara prefers working toward goals, being decisive, and setting deadlines; Larry, as a P (Perceiving), prefers to see how things develop and enjoys the process without much concern for when things get done. The Thinking/Feeling difference means that Larry tends to make decisions on the basis of what is fair, logical, and just, while Barbara tends to make decisions on the basis of the extenuating circumstances, the needs of the people, and what would create greatest harmony.

Larry and Barbara have been working together five years and generally have a smooth staff relationship. Larry values Barbara as a colleague and finds that she often has helpful insights concerning the church or people. Barbara appreciates Larry's sensitivity and willingness to listen carefully to what she has to say. They consider their staff relationship a good one. A recent incident, however, has caused them to reevaluate their relationship.

Larry knocked on the door of Barbara's office to ask her a question about a new Bible study program that was to begin on Sunday. As soon as Barbara invited him in, he realized that she had been crying.

When Larry asked what was wrong, Barbara began crying again. She explained that she had been talking to the new D.S. (district superintendent) about the upcoming National Lay Leaders Conference. She had volunteered to lead a program and was upset by his lack of enthusiasm. "I somehow don't feel that he respects me or thinks that I am competent," she said.

Larry did not know how to respond. He could not believe that the D.S. could feel that way. At the same time, he knew that Barbara did not make hasty judgments about people, especially if those judgments were negative. "Do you think this happened because you are a woman?" he asked.

"Well," Barbara started, "I don't know. I've wondered about that. Would he have ignored my offer if I were a man? Sometimes I wonder if I am just imagining the whole thing. I start out by getting mad at the D.S., and then I end up feeling that maybe I'm not as good as I think I am. Why do I always end up questioning myself?"

As they talked together, Larry tried to assure Barbara of her competence. The conversation, however, became more and more strained. Larry did not know what to say, and Barbara was embarrassed by what she felt was a bid for sympathy and an inappropriate demand on their professional relationship. Eventually the conversation shifted to the upcoming Bible study.

For Larry and Barbara to function as colleagues, it is vital that they each reveal their concerns about their self-worth instead of concentrating only on Barbara's struggles.

Just what is self-esteem? How does it relate to gender? How is self-esteem likely to affect male-female staff relationships? How is self-esteem influenced by our social systems, that is, our family of origin, our current systems of family, our educational institutions, our government, our parish, the larger church, and our church staff?

Self-esteem is the reputation that we have with ourselves.[1] Self-esteem is not an inappropriate pride in our accomplishments, but it is a healthy self-respect that allows us to use in ministry whatever gifts we have been given. Self-esteem, or the lack of it, affects our behavior and our relationships.[2]

We draw our self-esteem from four primary sources: (1) having visible achievements and accomplishing our goals, objectives, and expectations; (2) seeing evidence of our personal power and influence over events and people; (3) experiencing a sense of being accepted, valued, and cared about as worthwhile people; and (4) exhibiting behavior that is consistent with our personal values and beliefs.[3]

We need all four sources of self-esteem in order to feel good about ourselves over the course of time. We can temporarily compensate for a failure of esteem from one source by concentrating our energies on the other sources. In the long run, however, we need to have all four sources of self-esteem in our lives for the sake of our emotional health.[4]

Our reflections on self-esteem need to be placed in a biblical and theological perspective. Our ultimate source of self-esteem comes from the knowledge that we are accepted and valued by God for who we are, not for what we have or do. We are "worthwhile" because we are redeemed, justified, made righteous by God in Christ. This is an important issue and one to which we will return later in this chapter as we look at how Larry and Barbara are struggling with their theological perspectives on self-esteem.

As a result of our being valued as daughters and sons of God, we are free to exhibit behavior that is consistent with our values and goals. We can act in ways that serve God and our neighbor.

With the self-esteem that comes from God's redemptive love and the empowerment from God to behave in ways that reflect our beliefs and values, we are then able to do two things: (1) set and accomplish goals and objectives and (2) use our power and influence wisely and creatively.

How do these ideas apply to Barbara's and Larry's situation?

Following the discussion about Barbara's encounter with the D.S., Barbara and Larry decided to take some practical steps to increase their self-esteem. They began by looking at ways in which they could accomplish some of their goals and objectives.

As one of those who score as J (Judging) on the MBTI, Barbara especially needed to have deadlines to work toward and goals to accomplish. After talking together, Barbara and Larry decided that she would take over the fund-raising drive and the educational planning committee. This would enhance Barbara's self-esteem by allowing her to set goals and deadlines for projects such as the completion of the fund-raising drive.

Larry was willing to live within deadlines, but he, as a P (Perceiving), preferred waiting to see how things would develop. He enjoyed working with the worship committee and seeing services evolve. When Barbara was made responsible for organizing many of the projects and setting deadlines, Larry received fewer complaints from the congregation about his procrastination, and his self-esteem has improved.

Barbara and Larry have also considered issues of power and influence and their relationship to self-esteem. They thought about the names by which they are known in the congregation. Larry was usually addressed as "Pastor Edwards," except in informal social situations, while Barbara was addressed by her first name. Although they addressed one another directly on a first-name basis, Larry began to refer to Barbara as "Pastor Jennings" when others were present. They felt that this would help communicate to the parish their perception of their mutual power and value.

When Barbara was given more opportunities for leadership, her power and her influence with the members of the congregation increased. She has been asked more frequently for her advice and insights, and her self-esteem has increased.

Larry, in turn, realized no loss of self-esteem when he delegated some of his authority to Barbara. He is still valued as a caring and compassionate person. Now that decisions are made by Barbara as well as by Larry, he is seen as more powerful and less indecisive than before. His self-esteem has improved because he has owned and used his power effectively.

In this process, the self-esteem of both Larry and Barbara has been affected by the staff system in which they work. A system is a group of people whose interactions with one another are always in the process of changing and evolving. Whether the system is a family, staff, or parish, a system is active and dynamic, not static and passive. As members of a staff system, Larry and Barbara do not exist in a vacuum, but rather function interdependently. A system has its own set of rules, roles, forms of communication, power structure, and ways of dealing with conflict.[5]

A primary quality of a system is homeostasis. Homeostasis means that the participants in the system strive to maintain a sense of balance or equilibrium in the system. When one member of the system changes, the rest of the members also have to change in order to find a new sense of balance or equilibrium in the system. Thus a staff or family system is like a mobile: when one part changes its position, the homeostasis of the whole system is upset. Because all the parts of the mobile are interconnected, when one part moves, all the rest of the parts move until they all find a new state of balance or homeostasis.

Larry and Barbara need to be aware of the power of homeostasis in their staff and parish. They need to know that as Barbara changes, Larry will change and the church secretary will change. In addition, as Barbara changes her behavioral patterns with the parishioners, they will behave differently toward her.

We understand the process of change by looking at a dance. When you dance with a person who changes his/her dance steps, you naturally alter your dance steps in order to adapt to your partner's change. While the change in the dance steps may initially be awkward, we both gradually find a new balance or new way of dancing that works for both of us.

As Barbara and Larry explore self-esteem issues, it will be helpful for them to schedule regular sessions when they can each evaluate their own performance and hear that evaluation examined by their partner in ministry. In the process, they will think about the way they solve problems, as well as observe and reflect on the manner in which they give and receive criticism. These activities will keep the issue of self-esteem in the open, thus diminishing its power as a silent enemy of partnership and ministry. AMN

Pride and Hiding

Throughout its history, the church has provided theological interpretations for what we have been calling issues of self-esteem. Larry and Barbara have a deep commitment to that history of theological interpretation and are also committed, as pastors, to bringing their theology into lively and life-giving dialogue with the women and men of St Matthew's. We may find it useful to take a closer look at how these two religious leaders deal theologically with issues of self-esteem.

As Barbara and Larry work on issues of self-esteem and leadership, they do so against the background of a tradition that defines pride as "the cardinal sin." They know themselves as called to trust, not in their own righteousness, but in the grace of God. They know that their performance, no matter how competent, cannot justify their existence.

Barbara, however, has been struck by the insight of feminist theologians that pride is not a good description for the religious problem she and her female parishioners face. Women are much more likely to suffer from the spiritual sin of hiding, or self-abnegation, a failure to own and exercise their created gifts to the fullest. As Barbara talks with the other women in the parish, she discovers many common threads in their experiences growing up. She finds that other women hid their ability as children while their brothers exercised their powers fully. (One study of 150 gifted children found that 65 percent of the girls hid their ability while only 15 percent of the boys did so.)[6] She notices that other women, too, tend to avoid risking ventures in which they may fail, preferring instead to stay in low-profile positions in which they can be sure of meeting all expectations.

Barbara is also discovering that other clergywomen find themselves in the dilemma with which she struggles: how do they exercise their competence while maintaining the collegial relationships they value so highly? Hiding their competence is one tempting way out. Those who choose that resolution may receive positive reinforcement from others both in the church and in the culture.

Barbara has been slowly coming to see that hiding her competence is no less acute a form of human sinfulness than pride. After she had completed her first year at St. Matthew's, she was delighted when the lay leader took her aside after church one morning and said, "Barbara, you're the glue that holds this church together." Her pleasure at the compliment faded as she began to wonder: was "glue" what she wanted to be? Barbara now feels that her "glue period," as she calls it, was really a result of overemphasizing the feminine tendency to focus on human connectedness, to attend to the complex bonds that hold people together, to underemphasize her need to define herself as her own person with her own unique contributions to offer.

While Larry finds his spiritual condition helpfully addressed by a traditional Christian message about sin and grace and a justification in which he can take no pride, Barbara has been telling him that her experience is different. She needs a clearer sense of her own created goodness and a clearer call to take the risk of exercising her gifts fully. For her, failure to do so is to fall into the sin of hiding.

Their conversation last week revealed their growing clarity that their religious needs are different. Barbara said to Larry, "The wonderful thing is that I am discovering that I am all right! Me, not some nice lady who keeps everybody happy." Larry said, "My discovery feels a little different: I'm not all right, but that's all right. I have a hunch that we are both in touch with the truth that's important for us."

For a woman, it may be crucial to become aware that she is not as inadequate as she thought she was, so that she can come out of hiding. A man's way of repenting and encountering grace may mean discovering that he is not quite as adequate as he hoped he was. A traditional Christian message about sin and grace and a justification in which he can take no pride may be just what he needs.

Between them, Barbara and Larry are finding ways to address this more complex view of the human condition in their ministry at St. Matthew's. In their preaching they are balancing an emphasis on justification by grace with a call to act, to risk, to engage boldly in the ventures of ministry to which Christians are called. They have encouraged the women's group to stop getting speakers for their monthly meetings and are helping the leaders to design ways instead to elicit and affirm the gifts of the members. In this way, Larry and Barbara are finding that their more carefully considered understanding of the human condition enriches their understanding of one another and their ministry with the women and men of St. Matthew's. CAH

Questions for Reflection and Discussion

1. *How does your self-esteem affect how you do ministry?*
2. *How does your self-esteem affect your staff relationships?*
3. *In what ways does your partnership in ministry have a positive or negative effect on your self-esteem?*
4. *What do you see to be the relationship between your self-esteem and how you communicate and lead?*
5. *What are the most important religious issues in self-esteem for you?*

NOTES

1. Linda Tshirhart Sanford and Mary Ellen Donovan, *Women and Self-Esteem* (Baltimore: Penguin Books, 1984).

2. D. S. Ryan, "Self-Esteem: An Operational Definition and Ethical Analysis," *Journal of Psychology and Theology* 11 (1983): 295–302.

3. Pete Bradshaw, *The Management of Self-Esteem* (Englewood Cliffs, NJ: Prentice-Hall, 1981).

4. Ibid.

5. Irene Goldenberg and Harold Goldenberg, *Family Therapy: An Overview* (Monterey, CA: Brooks/Cole Publishing Co., 1980), 3.

6. *USA Today,* 25 February 1986; cited in *Daughters of Sarah* (September/October 1986), 30

Leadership

We now turn from the more internal issues of self-esteem to consider more objective issues concerning the structure and posture of leadership in the congregation. In addition to a senior pastor, church staffs may include other clergy and perhaps a lay professional and an administrative assistant. The leadership structure in which these people work is either hierarchical, collaborative, independent, or a combination of those styles.

Hierarchical Staff Structures

Hierarchically structured staffs, sometimes referred to as dependent staffs, are led by a senior pastor who is the clearly identified decision-maker. The head-of-staff makes all policy decisions, sets staff goals, and directs the staff in all of their tasks. While the advice of staff members about decisions and goals may be solicited, the staff do not have major influence in shaping those decisions and goals. Any decisions made at the staff level are subject to review by the higher authority of the senior pastor.[1] The expected behavior of staff members is to conform.[2]

The advantages of hierarchical staffs are their efficiency and the ability to make decisions and get things done quickly.[3] If the senior pastor is capable and respected, the staff members also possess a strong sense of purpose and accomplishment.[4]

The main disadvantages of the hierarchical structure are that the staff members tend to lack commitment to the goals and tend to lack interest or investment in the programs.[5] They are motivated by rewards or threats of punishment rather than by the work itself. Hierarchical staff structures do not facilitate staff unity or commitment because the senior pastor may either make personal

comments about and criticisms of the staff or avoid becoming
personally involved with them. Although hierarchical ways of
working are useful when an enterprise needs a high degree of
integration, hierarchical working structures often produce low
morale, a low level of unity among staff, diminished creativity, and
counterdependence—the "underlings" love to see the "top dog" in
the hierarchy "get it"!

Collaborative Staff Structures

In the collaborative staff structure, there are no independent
decisions; instead, every decision is referred to the staff team.[6] A
senior pastor working in a collaborative structure facilitates the
decision-making process within the staff, acts as a resource person,
and encourages decisions through staff consensus. Staff goals are
established by the staff and therefore shared fully by all members;
thus, there are no individual failures or successes, only staff failures
or staff successes.[7] Criticism tends to focus on facts rather than
persons, and the senior pastor is involved in the staff as a team
member.

The advantages of the collaborative staff structure are that this
style of leadership produces high morale, a high level of ownership
and investment, enhanced creativity, and healthy interdependence
and sharing of responsibility among the staff.[8]

The main disadvantages of this leadership style are that it takes a
great deal of time and can inhibit individual initiative and creativity
if one staff member's interests differ from those of the rest of the
staff.[9]

Independent Staff Structures

The senior pastor and staff members in independent staff structures
function quite separately from one another.[10] The senior pastor
gives staff members total freedom in their decision-making process
and in their tasks and activities. The leader functions as a resource
person if asked, does not criticize, and does not take part in the
tasks of the group. A church staff operating from this approach
usually does not have staff meetings, and staff members do not
interact with each other frequently.[11]

The independent staff structure has its advantages: there is the
potential for much creativity and freedom, and staff members do
not work under the constraint of constantly being watched or told

what to do.[12] If staff members have the same goals and their work integrates well, their staff relationship and ministry can be very productive.[13]

The independent staff structure can, however, foster conflict because individual staff members more easily build their own competitive following in the parish.[14] Independent structures offer little opportunity for expressing caring concern among the staff members and little opportunity to arrive at common staff goals.[15]

The morale, motivation, self-esteem, creativity, and job satisfaction of clergy are affected by the nature and function of the leadership structures of the multiple staff system. Multiple staffs in the church experience self-esteem and job satisfaction when the leadership styles are independent or collaborative and when everyone has power, more than when one person alone exercises power in the hierarchical style.[16]

Barbara and Larry work together in a staff system that incorporates both the collaborative and independent leadership structures. Although a collaborative style would find its fullest expression in a co-pastorate, Larry and Barbara are both committed to working collaboratively as much as possible within the confines of their positions as senior and associate pastors. Sharing areas of responsibility and decision making helps both of them feel that they are worthwhile members of the team.

Because of the pressures of time, however, Barbara and Larry end up working more independently than collaboratively on many projects. As is typical in independent leadership structures, Barbara has been given full responsibility in particular areas of ministry. In this independent leadership structure, Barbara feels increasingly more positive about herself and satisfied with her position as associate pastor. AMN

Leadership Postures

In this time of rapid change, many male-female staff teams find themselves caught between their values about leadership and the structures of the ecclesiastical organization in which they work. Katherine Myers and Paul Chin share a high value for equality and collaboration. They want to work as colleagues, and they are working hard to build the kinds of collegial relationships with the laity at Westminster Presbyterian Church that they believe will empower lay women and men for their ministries as they move out from the church into the world. Katherine and Paul want to share ministry and authority with lay leaders because they believe the ministry of the church is expanded by so doing and because they see positions of leadership within the congregation as a training ground for Christian leadership in families, in the workplace, and in the community.

But Paul and Katherine work in a church where the Session has mandated that their relationship be that of senior minister and associate. The organizational reality at Westminster Church is that the buck stops with the senior minister and that Katherine's job description requires her to report to Paul. When Katherine first talked to Paul about coming to Westminster, she liked what Paul said about "team ministry" and "collaboration." When she began work as associate, however, she was confused and frustrated when she began to discover that the church was not structured to support teamwork and collaboration but to maintain Paul's position and Katherine's in a one-up/one-down/ relationship. After a period of some confusion, misery, and growing distrust, Katherine and Paul are learning how to distinguish the organizational realities over which they do not have control from both their own values about collaboration and the power they do have to influence others toward structural changes that support collaboration. The discomfort has not disappeared, but they are learning to address and analyze some of the problems. Katherine says, "I prefer to think of our relationship as one of equals rather than one of hierarchy, but the bottom line is that he is in a position to offer me directives. He is responsible for church staff oversight."

Paul struggles with the disjuncture between the prescribed organizational relationship and the more egalitarian work relationship he, too, would prefer. "How do I give direction without being perceived as authoritarian or chauvinistic?" he wonders. "I don't feel comfortable giving marching orders, but I do want to exercise the authority of my role. I get self-conscious about the possibility of becoming overbearing as *male, senior* minister, *supervisor*." Paul's growing curiosity about these hard questions and his willingness to ask Katherine how his leadership style affects her combine to provide some answers to his dilemma.

Paul's and Katherine's new clarity about the distinction between values and organizational requirements helps them to be more honest with one another. They are also finding ways to change parts of the structure.

Katherine and Paul have spent some time discussing the various aspects of their jobs in which different working relationships might be appropriate. Some of the time their working roles are related hierarchically; this fits with the church structure and saves time. They teach a Bible class in which they function collaboratively.

Their planning sessions for the class take a lot of time, but these hours of preparation help them grow and lay the groundwork for modeling in class sessions the kind of collaboration they see as empowering for lay people. In still other parts of the work, such as Katherine's youth ministry, their style of working has a more independent character, which again saves planning time and allows Katherine areas for exercising her own creativity and taking the responsibility to plan and carry out a complete program.

While Paul and Katherine agree that their preferred leadership posture is not that of being "set over" one another or the members of Westminster Church, they have become aware that their leadership postures differ in other ways. Paul is more likely to see himself as "set apart" from parishioners, while Katherine prefers to see herself as "set alongside" those with whom she ministers. Paul has been discovering that Edwin H. Friedman's treatment of leadership in *Generation to Generation: Family Process in Church and Synagogue*[17] has articulated his instincts in helpful ways. Friedman advocates "leadership by self-differentiation" as a helpful alternative to authoritarian or consensus leadership styles, both of which bind the leader and the group together. The authoritarian leader compels the group to go along with him, and the consensus leader in effect joins the group. Leaders can take another approach that Friedman believes works better: Be yourself. Define yourself and state your positions clearly, thus encouraging followers, too, in self-definition as they make their own determination of how to respond to the leader. This model of set-apart leadership helps Paul voice his beliefs clearly and delegate responsibilities cleanly, allowing volunteers to own their own successes and failures. When no one came forward to chair the annual Mission Auction, Paul thought carefully. Every year he seemed to spend days on the phone recruiting for that event. Paul decided he was overfunctioning and determined it would be most helpful to allow the parish to experience a year with no auction.

Katherine has a different approach to leadership. She tends to stress her connectedness with people in the parish rather than the distinctiveness of her role,[18] positioning herself as leader alongside those she leads. When leading classes, she likes to work with a partner, believing that this indicates an openness to the leadership of class members as well. She habitually arranges the chairs in a circle and often designs sessions in which every participant will have time to tell his or her story. In summarizing a session, she likes to use the group members' own words to gather up what they learned. When Katherine visited a terminally ill cancer patient, she found the woman's prayer and support group present and invited them to join her in a brief ritual of laying-on-of-hands and prayers. When Katherine herself had two weeks in bed following surgery last year, she found herself welcoming the visits, casseroles, and help with carpools and errands provided by members of the parish. They, in turn, found this period of ministering to the minister significant in their own spiritual growth.

Katherine's recent evaluation indicated that parishioners appreciate her easy relationship with them and her desire to incorporate other people into the decision making. But some said they wanted her to be a more assertive leader. Her leadership style does not fit some members' pictures of what a leader should do. She will have to assess both her own style and those expectations and then determine what part of the criticism reflects expectations that are foreign to Katherine's style and what part points to ways toward which she may decide to shift her way of leading.

While Katherine and Paul both delegate responsibilities clearly, they agree that the emphasis in their ministries is not identical. Both affirm the strengths of their own stance, but each also learns from the other. Katherine has profited from Paul's steady encouragement to define herself and her pastoral style. Paul is grateful for the permission he receives from Katherine to acknowledge areas in which he feels shaky and to ask for support when he needs it. Parishioners benefit from pastoral leadership that brings set-apart and set-alongside postures together, and that thereby points to the transcendence and immanence of God. CAH

The Effect of Power

We cannot explore leadership without asking, What is power? Staff relationships are significantly affected by how each of the members of the staff chooses to share power and leadership. When we understand power as the *experience* of *feeling strength* and power, *we are less likely to use power to dominate others.*[19] When Barbara and Larry both *claim* their personal power, they enhance their self-esteem and their staff relationship. When they *feel* their power, they interact with each other from positions of strength—sharing, listening, discussing, and differing.

Men and women view power differently.[20] Barbara is representative of many women in that she wants to be powerful and strong in order to have and share resources with others, while Larry is representative of many men in that he wants to act powerfully in order to influence others.[21] Yet clergymen are not necessarily representative of men in our culture: some clergymen do want power in order to influence and persuade, but other clergymen want power in order to help empower others. In one study of multiple staff relationships, slightly more than fifty percent of the clergymen and eighty percent of the clergywomen preferred having power in order to have and share resources with others.[22]

Historically it was the role of the ordained pastor to resolve conflicts and any other issues that congregational members faced in their personal lives. In this power structure, the pastor as "paterfamilias" could exercise near absolute authority over the lives of the members of his congregation. Many people continue to look to male pastors for this type of patriarchal leadership.

It is no wonder that Barbara senses some people's discomfort with her role as pastor at times. Women may not fit comfortably into patriarchal models of leadership. Either they will not be effective leaders because they are unable to be effective "fathers," or they will find themselves uncomfortable with the incongruence be-tween a role as defined by men and their authentic self. In the culture in which we live, femininity and power are at times seen as incompatible with one another. Yet, through facing such issues head-on, clarifying their own inner convictions, and talking openly with one another, women and men can work together to the end that women and men can become full partners in ministry.

Women are changing the church power structures by entering the clergy ranks and bringing new views of power, leadership, and decision-making processes. A few women are beginning to serve as senior ministers, co-pastors, pastors, and rectors. In our regional and national church bodies a few women are being elected to influential church offices and commissions, and some women are serving as executive presbyters, bishops, and district superintendents. In such positions, women may be changing the power structures by joining with men in the leadership. As men and women share as partners and leaders in ministry, we will create new leadership styles that combine feminine and masculine gifts and hold promise for vitalizing our ministries. AMN

Power and Vulnerability

From boyhood on, men are taught to claim their power. This emphasis on *agency,* with its willingness to reach out and move forward, is in many ways a gift. A man's claiming of power affirms life. The act of claiming is positive. It enables him to be intentional about life for himself and for others.

Often, however, the courage of the combatant is bought at the price of pushing down and out of sight those other inescapable realities of human life—our fear, weakness, and vulnerability. Vulnerability tends to grate against a man's sense of himself as a man. As Mark Gerzon puts it, "I never saw John Wayne walk up to a woman and say, 'I need a hug.' "[23] Yet claiming power and denying vulnerability has its downside for a man and for the women with whom he interacts. The man who is stuck in self-sufficiency may push himself too hard and fail to get his needs met; he is a good candidate for burnout. The need to maintain an image of power may lead men to constrict their emotional self-expression, to keep secrets from women and from other men. Refusing to engage women, to dignify their challenges with a response, or to give them straight feedback can be an effective strategy for preserving male power and making change more difficult for both men and women.

Both men and women live in the tension between vulnerability and power. While men tend to avoid vulnerability, women often have trouble accepting their own power. Because their bodies give them graceful lessons in letting happen what needs to happen, women sometimes show a paradoxical strength as they embrace their vulnerability. While men are more likely to deny what is out of control, women more easily surrender possibilities of taking control. A woman may avoid positions of power as an easy way to be innocent. Or she may quickly give up her ground when a male co-worker's negative response leads her to conclude that any use of her power will be destructive. One way to risk showing power is through expressing anger. Yet anger is often seen as unacceptable for clergy, and people become particularly uncomfortable when confronted by angry women.

Men find it easier to say, "I can do it"; women more easily conclude, "I can't"—yet *both* realities mark the experience of every human being. As we reach toward maturity we may be liberated from the temptation to throw out whichever half of this paradoxical reality—the "I can" or the "I can't"—makes us uncomfortable. Both men and women may live more deeply into the insights that power exercised in loving service is the only kind that works, and that our power is made perfect in weakness. Little by little, each of us may learn to decide more freely when it is time to reach out with energy and initiative, and when we need to wait, trust, and discern when "the fullness of time" is upon us.

Clergy, in a calling shaped by male perceptions of reality, are subject to a variety of seductions (sometimes subtle) to present themselves as invulnerable. The dynamics in the relationship between clergy and laity intensify the temptation from both sides. The myth of "the holy man" is alive and well in our churches. It goes like this: "God has set aside a special group of people who are not ordinary humans but who have godlike qualities of moral perfection, freedom from temptation and sinfulness and who are possessed with a special wisdom. These men...can answer all questions and solve all problems."[24] One of the clergymen Barbara Gilbert interviewed said, "If as the helper I need help, then what kind of a helper am I?"

Understandable fears exacerbate the temptation to grasp the role of the holy man. Clergy are hired leaders in a not-totally-rational system. They know they are the stand-in objects of deep yearnings and transcendent hopes. People would like their religious leaders to be more powerful than human beings can ever be.

Though the temptations for clergy to present themselves as helpers who themselves require no help are sometimes overwhelming, those who succumb are likely to find that they have surrendered their power as religious leaders. Clergy who hang on to the holy man myth and hide all their weaknesses are unlikely to invite their parishioners to reveal the vulnerable and broken dimensions of their lives. Most of us feel distinctly disinclined to open up our guilty and sore spots to someone who appears to have everything under control.

Then, too, as Barbara Gilbert points out, clergy who claim the seemingly benign "helper" posture assign their parishioners the needy role of "helpee," thus perpetuating dominant/subordinate relationships, disempowering the laity, and cutting themselves off from the support lay people might offer if they thought their pastors needed it. And so we end up with burned-out clergy and laity who fall into the role of patients. Clergy who present themselves only as competent helpers not only disempower those they are charged to empower, but also fail to serve as authentic examples of the dependence on God they preach about on Sunday mornings.

In contrast, religious leaders, clergy or lay, who stand in the tension between power and vulnerability will invite others to claim both realities in their own lives. Last fall the district superintendent invited Larry to lead a workshop on how clergy can collaborate more with laity. Many of the pastors came to this event feeling nervous about letting go of any of the prerogatives of their role. As one finally asked, "If I let the lay people take on more and more leadership, what will *my* job be?" Larry disarmed the pastors by telling them of several mistakes he had made in his experiments with more collaborative leadership. The group immediately relaxed; Larry's openness enabled them to begin looking at the promises they imagined more mutual styles might hold and to plan ways to exercise collaborative strengths in their own parishes.

Vulnerable leaders lead us into religious power. And when churches help people know their own power instead of teaching them that they are powerless, the ministry of the laity becomes a reality instead of a pious hope. When clergy see their role as equipping the saints instead of *being* the saints,[25] they can invite lay men and women to join them as companions in ministry.

Barbara and Larry are also more effective in encouraging the members of St. Paul's to embrace both their power and their vulnerability because they are aware that men and women may have different religious needs. Christian theology has focused on correcting men's reliance on power and denial of vulnerability. If the church can attend to the needs of women as well, it will provide them with religious undergirding for their struggle to discover and claim their strength.

Thus the ministry of the male-female team holds the possibilities of enriching the life of the whole church. As women and men begin to share more equally in religious leadership, men will share with female colleagues their greater sophistication in the uses of power and will find healing from the stresses of having always to stay in control. Claiming their strength, women will also offer their gifts, which include a trustful relaxing into the darkness, a yielding to the power that undergirds all human vulnerability. CAII

Questions for Reflection and Discussion

1. *What shared and differing convictions does your church staff have about leadership styles?*
2. *What steps might you take to see that those similarities or differences work well for the parish?*
3. *"Meaningful power in a congregation is. . . ." Complete the sentence. Think of a recent incident in which you exercised that kind of power.*
4. *Is it harder for you to claim power or to acknowledge vulnerability?*

NOTES

1. Anne Marie Nuechterlein, *Strengthening the Multiple Staff* (Minneapolis: American Lutheran Church, 1982).

2. Ibid.

3. Ibid.

4. Ibid.

5. Ibid.

6. Ibid.

7. Ibid.

8. Speed B. Leas, lecture presented at Male-Female Staff Teams Conference in Annapolis, Maryland sponsored by The Alban Institute, 1986.

9. Nuechterlein, op. cit.

10. Ibid.

11. Leas, op. cit.

12. Nuechterlein, op cit.

13. Ibid.

14. Ibid.

15. Ibid.

16. Anne Marie Nuechterlein, "Multiple Staff Clergy Relationships" (Ph.D. diss., Texas Woman's University, 1986).

17. Edwin H. Friedman, *Generation to Generation: Family Process in Church and Synagogue* (New York: Guilford Press, 1985).

18. Carol Gilligan, *In a Different Voice: Psychological Theory and Women's Development* (See Notes, Chap. I).

19. D. McClelland, *Power: The Inner Experience* (New York: John Wiley and Sons, 1975).

20. Nuechterlein, diss.; A. J. Stewart and D. G. Winter, "Arousal of the Power Motive in Woman," *Journal of Consulting and Clinical Psychology* 44 (1984): 495–96.

21. McClelland, op. cit.

22. Nuechterlein, diss., op. cit.

23. Mark Gerzon, *A Choice of Heroes* (Boston: Houghton Mifflin, 1982), 3.

24. Clyde Reid, cited in Barbara Gilbert, *Who Ministers to Ministers* (Washington, DC: The Alban Institute, 1987), 38.

25. Gilbert, op. cit., 44

CHAPTER IV

Roles

Women have only recently begun to occupy professional positions of equal status with men, and these "equal" positions have been often lacking in comparable authority, power, prestige, status, and salary.[1] While Susan and Charles are both ordained clergy, Charles holds the position of senior pastor and therefore occupies the position with higher authority, status, salary, prestige, and power. Susan's position in relation to Charles's position is typical of most clergywomen's positions in relation to those of their male ordained colleagues.

While some women have been solo pastors with their own churches, Susan and Barbara are like many clergywomen who have been able to find positions only as associate pastors. Institutional sexism has limited Julie's roles too.[2] Julie Everson served as the pastor of a small, rural parish in Wisconsin. After five years as a solo pastor, she received a call to be a co-pastor with a male pastor in Milwaukee. Julie has discovered that even though they are co-pastors, her male colleague is obviously seen as having more authority.

Many believe that clergywomen now have equal status with clergymen, but the reality is that women have a much more difficult time than men in obtaining parish positions, and the positions are often not equal in authority, prestige, status, salary, or power.[3]

Traditional Sex Roles

Many male and female clergy do not take on traditional sex roles. But many of us—often on an unconscious level—expect ourselves and each other to take on traditional sex roles. As you read this section, think about your own sex role in your staff, as well as the sex roles of your colleagues. What fits and does not fit for your staff?

Susan has found that she often takes on the traditional feminine role of being emotional or expressive. She believes that she tends to occupy the role of the considerate, affective, and tactful member of the staff, instead of taking on instrumental roles that are task- and achievement-oriented.

Susan's friend, Jo-Ellen Hardy, an associate in the United Church of Christ church nearby, has had quite a different experience. As an INTJ, she has strong conceptual gifts and a clear sense of her own authority. Jo-Ellen's annual evaluation yielded some criticism that she was not proving to be the warm, accessible, easygoing youth worker that her ENFP predecessor had been. Jo-Ellen may need to think over what part of this criticism arises from members' expectations that she will exhibit feminine, "set-alongside" strengths and what part is related to her personality type. She will need to assess the expectations, her own strengths, and her needs to grow in ministry with young people.

Charles has found that he is more likely to take on masculine roles that emphasize being task-oriented, competent, and achievement-oriented, instead of taking on emotional roles that call for being sensitive. Because of cultural conditioning, women are generally more likely to take on socioemotive and expressive roles and men are generally more likely to take on task and instrumental roles related to competence, power, and achievement.[4]

An additional result of cultural conditioning is that women are not as likely as men to imagine themselves as future leaders. The sex of the leader and the sex composition of a group significantly affect how the leader performs and how the group members interact with each other.[5] Partly because of their socialization, men have higher occupational status overall and are encouraged to be leaders in small, mixed-sex groups, while women tend to have lower status and are encouraged to have a more supportive, emotional role.[6]

Barbara recognizes that she, as a woman, has been socially and culturally conditioned to be actively involved in service projects and behind-the-scenes church work that have called forth socioemotive roles. She recognizes further that she generally has not been encouraged to take on masculine roles and be a leader of a church group or of churches.[7]

Larry believes that he was socially and culturally conditioned from an early age to be actively involved in the leadership of the church. His teachers, pastors, and parents encouraged him to be a pastor or missionary. From the time he was a young boy, he was encouraged to be an achiever and a leader in the church and thereby take on the masculine roles of competence, achievement, authority, and strength.

Masculinity and femininity have traditionally been seen as opposite polarities, with people having the option of being either masculine or feminine, but not both. Psychologically masculine people tend to choose instrumental roles involving competence or achievement, while people who are more psychologically feminine choose socioemotive roles.[8]

Women and men in ministry tend toward psychological androgyny; that is, they experience the integration of both masculine and feminine qualities. Psychologically androgynous people choose behavior patterns that are both instrumental (task- and achievement-oriented) and socioemotive (emotional and expressive).[9] They are usually able to be both assertive and compassionate, instrumental and expressive, exercising masculine or feminine strengths depending on the needs of the immediate situation.[10]

During their weekly staff meeting, Charles and Susan somehow began discussing how healthy it was for clergy to have both masculine and feminine qualities. Charles knew that he wanted to be more aware of his feminine side, but he was not sure he wanted to discuss something so personal. But then he thought, Earl just died of a heart attack at the age of fifty-four. Life is too short for me not to deal with this stuff. I really admired Earl, and I want to be more like him. Charles decided to go ahead and speak with Susan about it.

He looked at her and said, "I've been thinking about this business of male clergy needing to allow their feminine qualities to be expressed and female clergy needing to allow their masculine qualities to be expressed. And I'm not sure about how to approach it. Earl's death has made me think about a lot of things, and I would like to be more like Earl—more sensitive to people, more people-oriented, more able to express feelings."

Susan was surprised at Charles's openness, but appreciated his willingness to confide in her. She asked, "How would you go about becoming more like Earl?"

Charles said, "I'd like to become more emotional and sensitive—not overly emotional—but more able to express my emotions. I always admired the gentle, sensitive, and caring way Earl related with people. But I also knew that everyone wanted me to be strong. I can still hear my parents saying, 'Stop being so sensitive' and 'Just keep busy and you'll be OK.' "

Susan said, "As we talk, I realize that I was also raised to be a certain way in order to be acceptable—in my case, I guess I'd say I was raised to be a 'nice young lady.' And I'd like to develop more of the so-called masculine qualities. I'd like to learn how to be more efficient and assertive in my work. I also need to express my opinions more and to be more direct with men when I'm upset."

Charles asked, "What do you mean?"

Susan said, "I think disagreeing with men is difficult for me because I was raised to always be pleasing and agreeable. Confronting people is hard for me, and confronting men is especially hard because I keep hearing my parents' voices saying, 'Nice girls never talk back,' 'Don't be so disagreeable,' and 'Always be pleasant and nice.' Somehow I always ended up apologizing for what I said, even if I had good reasons for being angry."

They talked for a few minutes about how Susan might go about learning to be more honest with men when she is upset. She asked Charles whether he noticed that she had been more assertive at the last council meeting.

Even though Charles had not noticed her efforts, Susan wanted to keep trying to express more masculine qualities such as authority and strength. She resolved to stand up for her convictions at the next council meeting.

Susan had noticed that Joe, the stewardship chairperson, seemed to disapprove of her developing assertiveness. While Joe applauded Charles's forceful statements at church council meetings, Susan believed that Joe patronized her when she expressed strong opinions or thoughts.

Susan and Charles made a pledge to one another. Susan told Charles that she would continue to work on being more assertive, and Charles told Susan that he would consciously try to express more sensitivity and warmth.

Susan liked the feminine side of who she was and knew that she brought a great deal of strength to her pastoral ministry through her feminine qualities. She thought, though, that her ministry would be more effective if she took on some of the masculine qualities of authority and assertiveness.

Charles, too, was aware that although he cherished his masculine qualities and found them a great asset in his ministry, he would be more effective if he developed more feminine qualities. He wanted to allow the feminine side of himself—his feelings, sensitivities, and warmth—to be more fully expressed in his ministry. By intentionally developing new qualities and new roles, Susan and Charles believed they would enhance their relationship and their ministry.

Psychological Roles in Staff Relationships

When Susan and Charles talk with one another about their roles, they are talking about the behavioral patterns people expect from them. These socially defined patterns are ways of acting that affect their staff relationship.[11]

All staff members have a role in the staff "family" by virtue of their gender, birth order, the staff authority system, their job description, and the particular staff system in which they work. The roles are maintained by the staff system as a means of keeping the system balanced. Thus, if your role is to be the peacemaker and you suddenly refuse to take on that role and instead become the comic, the staff and work system are thrown off balance and into some kind of struggle or crisis.[12]

Groups that are dedicated to avoiding conflicts often choose a woman on the staff to "be the pourer of oil on troubled waters."[13] Neither Charles nor Susan were comfortable with conflict, and Susan has served as peacemaker in their staff relationship. As long as she maintained that role in their system, the system appeared to function well.

While women are often chosen to be the peacemakers, men are often elected to be in charge of the rituals. According to Kenneth Mitchell, as long as "women had only a small or an indirect hand in the architecture of ritual, the extent of their influence could be kept under masculine control."[14] Issues of ritual and control may be important reasons why women are seldom senior pastors and tend to be in an employee role rather than in the role of authority as clergy.

Staff members often unconsciously choose women to express feelings for the group.[15] At St. Matthew's, Barbara expressed emotions more freely than Larry and believed that she was the one in her staff who was chosen to be the "emotion bearer." Having been raised with four older brothers and no sisters, she believed that she had been chosen to take on this role in her family of origin. Thus, it was natural to accept this familiar role given by her work family.

Birth Order Roles

Barbara was the youngest girl with four older brothers. Larry was the oldest boy of five children. He had four sisters and no younger brothers. The way Larry and Barbara experienced their relationship with each other is closely related to their birth order roles. Birth order influences the personality characteristics of 70 to 80 percent of the adult population.[16] Birth order is one factor to consider in selecting new staff and in further developing staff relationships.[17]

Birth order roles and gender roles describe how people in sibling positions usually function. Once staff members understand that a component of their staff difficulties may be related to their birth order roles, they have a clear frame of reference to use as they explore how they need to compromise, adapt, and change in order for their staff relationships to function well.

Birth order roles are determined by one's position in the family, one's gender, the number of siblings one has, and their ages. The oldest boy in a family with all boys has a different role than the oldest boy in a family with all girls. An oldest boy and an oldest girl have different characteristics as well.

After a five and one half-year gap between children, the birth order roles in a family system begin again. For example, if I am the oldest child and I have a brother two years younger and a sister eight years younger, my brother is like a youngest child and my sister is like an only child. In some families, there will be two separate families of children: three children less than five years apart from one another, a gap of over five and one half years, and another group of children relatively close together in age.

Working on staffs composed of people with different birth orders and gender roles tends to be less stressful and tumultuous than working on staffs with the same birth order. For example, an oldest sister of brothers usually works quite well with a youngest brother of sisters because both people are comfortable with re-creating role patterns they experienced as children. A staff member finds it comfortable to work with someone who is in a birth order and gender role similar to that of the staff member's sibling. In such staff relationships, the birth order and gender roles are familiar to staff members. Thus they know how to act with one another, and it is generally not necessary to learn new patterns of interaction. Even if unhappy in their roles in their families of origin, people are more comfortable in duplicating the birth order and gender role constellations they knew as children than they are in learning new birth order and gender roles.

It is possible to work with someone of the same birth order and have a well-functioning staff relationship. But working with people of the same birth order role often involves more energy and much more work because both people are competing for the same roles in their working relationship.

The most difficult working relationship is when at least two of the staff are oldest children.[18] Oldest children tend to be responsible, serious, achievement-oriented, and accustomed to being in charge. Oldest children working with other oldest children often struggle over who is in charge and who will have the final responsibility. An oldest sister of sisters and an oldest brother of brothers find it particularly difficult to work together because neither is accustomed to relating with people of the other sex.

In addition, the larger the family, the more firmly siblings are entrenched in their birth order roles. If two oldest children working together each have five younger siblings, their birth order and gender roles are firmly established, and they are likely to have conflicts. If the oldest children working together both have one or two younger siblings, their birth order and gender roles are less strongly established, and they are less likely to have conflicts than oldest children from larger families.

The second most difficult working relationship occurs when at least two of the staff are youngest children.[19] Youngest children tend to be playful, optimistic, creative, easygoing, and unambitious, and they are more likely to be followers than leaders. Two youngest children working together on a church staff often find themselves vying for the same role of being playful, dependent, and a follower. A church staff composed only of youngest children often experiences both a lack of decisive leadership and competition between two staff members who want to be taken care of by another staff member.

Two youngest children can have a well-functioning staff relationship, but they will need to work much harder at their relationship than an oldest and a youngest child serving together. By examining their roles as youngest children, they can come to terms with their tendencies to want to be taken care of and to be followers rather than leaders.

Barbara, as the youngest girl of a family composed primarily of boys, has a birth order role significantly different from that of Larry, who was the oldest brother of four girls. Their complementary birth order roles helped their staff relationship function harmoniously most of the time.

As a youngest sister of boys, Barbara is used to being around males, feels comfortable with men, and relates easily to them. As a youngest sister of brothers, she is fun-loving, optimistic, and easygoing. At times, she can be self-centered because her father and older brothers spoiled her a bit. At the same time, she can be passive and submissive because that was the role she took on as the daughter and youngest sister. As a youngest sister of brothers, she is more comfortable working as an assistant or associate pastor with a male senior pastor than she would be working as a solo pastor or as a senior pastor.

Larry, as the oldest brother of sisters, is comfortable with women and kind and thoughtful toward them. His good relationship with Barbara may in part be due to their birth order roles. He had younger sisters and Barbara is a younger sister, which means that it is easy for both Larry and Barbara to re-create their birth order roles from their families of origin. Larry likes working with women and prefers being the leader. He very much enjoys being the senior pastor in a staff composed primarily of women, although he has to take care to avoid being either patronizing or paternalistic. He would not be as comfortable working as an assistant or associate pastor.[20]

As men and women sharing in ministry, we are confronted with challenges and creative opportunities to discover and shape our roles on the staff and in pastoral leadership. Through individual and group reflection on sex roles, psychological roles, and birth order and gender roles, we can develop increased insight and make new choices about who we are as women and men working together in parish staff relationships.

By reflecting on our sex roles and the social and cultural conditioning that goes along with them, we can make intentional decisions about the roles that we want to choose now. After examining our psychological roles, we can better understand how we relate with one another, and what is healthy or unhealthy about our particular roles as "peacemaker," "responsible one," or "the comic." Through exploring our birth order and gender roles, we can also gain insight into our staff relationships and come up with some specific, concrete ideas about how to better relate with each other. With an understanding of each other's sex roles, psychological roles, and birth order and gender roles, as well as a mutual concern for the development of each other's personhood, we will enliven our partnerships and enhance our ministries. AMN

Questions for Reflection and Discussion:

1. *What roles do you tend to assume in your staff relationship?*
2. *What roles do you perceive your teammate(s) assuming in your staff relationships?*
3. *What was your birth order role in your family of origin? What were your colleagues' birth order roles in their families of origin?*
4. *What dimensions of who you are as an oldest, only, second,*

middle, or youngest child are an asset in your staff relationships? What dimensions are a struggle for you in your staff relationships?

5. *How do your colleagues' roles complement your team relationships? How do your and your colleagues' roles detract from the smooth functioning of your staff relationships?*

NOTES

1. B. Powell and J. A. Jacobs, "The Prestige Gap: Differential Evaluations of Male and Female Workers," *Work and Occupations* 11 (1984): 383–398.

2. E. C. Lehman, "Placement of Men and Women in the Ministry," *Review of Religious Research* 22 (1980): 18–40 (p. 1 Institutional sexism has limited. . .).

3. K. Flagg, "Psychological Androgyny and Self-esteem in Clergywomen," *Journal of Psychology and Theology* 12 (1984): 222–229.

4. S. Shichman and E. Cooper, "Life Satisfaction and Sex-role Concept," *Sex Roles* 11 (1984): 227–40.

5. A. Eskilson and M. G. Wiley, "Sex Composition and Leadership in Small Groups," *Sociometry* 39 (1976): 183–94.

6. E. S. Thune, R. Manderscheid, and S. Silberfeld, "Status or Sex Roles as Determinants of Interaction Patterns in Small, Mixed-sex Groups," *The Journal of Social Psychology* 112 (1980): 51–65.

7. K. R. Mitchell, *Multiple Staff Ministries* (Philadelphia: Westminster Press, 1988).

8. Shichman and Cooper, op. cit.

9. Ibid.

10. A. B. Heilbrun, "Measurement of Masculine and Feminine Sex Role Identities as Independent Dimensions," *Journal of Consulting and Clinical Psychology* 44 (1976): 183–90.

11. Irene Goldenberg and Harold Goldenberg, *Family Therapy: An Overview* (Monterey, CA: Brooks/Cole Publishing, 1980).

12. Anne Marie Nuechterlein, *Improving Your Multiple Staff Ministry* (Minneapolis: Augsburg, 1989), 60.

13. Mitchell, op. cit.

14. Ibid.

15. Walter Toman, *Family Constellations* (New York: Springer Publishing, 1976).

16. Ibid.

17. L. E. Schaller, *The Multiple Staff and the Local Church* (Nashville: Abingdon, 1980).

18. Ibid.

19. Ibid.

20. Toman, op. cit

CHAPTER V

Communication

How do we communicate with each other? Do we communicate as "experts" through a "top-down" process, or do we communicate as "colleagues" through a "dialogue" process? How does communication affect our sense of self, our relationships as women and men? What is the connection between communication and power?

Communicating as a Top-Down Process

"One more thing," Ray Odenino, the senior pastor at Christ Church, said to his new associate, Donna Rafferty. "This first year you'll be in charge of the youth activities."

Donna could not believe she was hearing right. She thought to herself, How on earth can he do this to me? We already agreed on this—he knows that I don't want to be in charge of the youth. She said, "I thought we had agreed that since I was not interested in youth work, you would have the new lay associate work with youth."

Ray said, "The lay associate is in his fifties and too old to work with youth. The young people and their parents would most certainly be happier if you were the youth director. You'll do a better job."

Donna said, "But even though I'm in my twenties and closer to their age, I really don't want to work with them. I thought we had agreed that he would be in charge of the youth. Can we talk about this?"

Ray said, "We have to move on to the rest of the agenda. I've decided that it would be best if you handled the youth—at least for this first year. I've worked with these young folks for years. I really know them and their parents, too. I am sure that they would much prefer working with you."

Donna left Ray's office furious. She could not believe that she was being told to work with youth after they had earlier reached a clear understanding that she would not work with them. Yet Ray's tone of voice had made it clear that the decision was not negotiable.

Ray communicated with Donna in a "top-down" manner. While she wanted to negotiate with him how the youth program could best be led, he wanted to tell her that she would be in charge of the youth. He was willing to discuss with her how she would lead the youth, but the question of whether she would lead them was not open for discussion.

Many people communicate through a top-down process. In the top-down communication style, the one who possesses knowledge communicates it down to others—teachers lecture, bosses give orders, managers inform employees, and preachers proclaim from the pulpit. Many of us, like Ray, are raised to communicate in this way—as "experts."[1]

There are advantages to top-down communication. As experts, we accept the responsibilities of being in authority; we may have special knowledge to convey or skills to teach. Communicating as an expert can be helpful when the situation requires that we tell others what we already know.

There are, however, disadvantages to constantly engaging in top-down communication as experts. If we must always be knowledgeable or in charge, we are not free to choose between top-down communication and dialogue. According to Mark Gerzon, author of *A Choice of Heroes: The Changing Face of American Manhood,* we experts, at our best, pursue truth. Many of us experts, however, use our minds to pursue power. People who know more have more power. Knowledge often is a commodity of power: those who have access to it are powerful; those who do not are powerless.[2] In addition, experts who thrive on being the authority do not recognize opportunities to learn something new.[3]

While there are appropriate times to communicate in this top-down style, in this case, Ray misused his power. Rather than use the top-down style of communication in a helpful way, Ray told Donna what he knew without any regard for her thoughts or insights. Because he did not listen to her or communicate *with* her, Ray's top-down communication style left Donna feeling hurt and angry. The next scene in this drama will probably feature a resentful associate minister, an angry or bored group of young people, and some disgruntled parents.

Ray took on the expert role with Donna to show her his power when he said, "I've worked with these young folks for years. I really know them and their parents, too. I am sure that they would much prefer working with you." Because her role was that of associate and she did not know the youth or their parents, she believed she was in a powerless position.

Like Ray, experts often discount, or are perceived to discount, people who disagree with them. They assume others do not have the knowledge necessary to make the right decisions. When we act like experts, we may not intend to discount others or set ourselves above them, but our stance as experts is seen by others as reflecting a belief that we are superior to the rest of the staff.

Communicating in a Dialogue Process

While the majority of us at times employ the top-down communication style, whether in appropriate or unhelpful ways, some of us are also able to use a "dialogue" communication style in which we seek to arrive at knowledge together. When we engage in dialogue together, we share our own experiences, thoughts, and feelings and listen to each other as well.

Craig Freeman and Jean Schultz, ministers at First Congregational United Church of Christ, were discussing how best to relate to the eight committees of the church for the upcoming year. Craig suggested that they each choose four committees for which they would have full responsibility. Jean smiled and said, "I'd love to do that. It would save time for both of us not to attend all the meetings, and it would convey a new image of partnership to our congregation."

As they discussed their preferences, Craig said that he had a slight preference for the education and stewardship committees, but was open to whatever committees Jean preferred. Jean said to Craig, "I'm pleased that we'll be sharing the committees, but I know that the senior minister often is in charge of stewardship, worship, and finance. Do you want to be in charge of those three committees?"

"Not necessarily," Craig said. "In fact, it would probably be good for you to have primary responsibility with a few of the committees that are usually led by the senior minister. That way the committee members and the congregational members can see our partnership and experience that you are in every way a minister."

Jean and Craig discussed their genuine interests and preferences with one another, dividing the responsibility for six committees with relative ease. The last two committees required more discussion. They both had a preference for the social ministry committee, and they both preferred not to work with the property committee. They decided to take turns, switching responsibility for these two committees each year.

Rather than talking to one another as experts, Craig and Jean engaged in dialogue as colleagues who talked *with* one another and listened to one another. To enter into dialogue, there must be a balance between talking and listening. Each person needs to speak with and listen to the other as well as speak with and listen to the self.[4]

Colleagues who engage in dialogue do not impart knowledge from the top down, but rather arrive at knowledge through "real talk." Craig and Jean engaged in real talk. Each asked for the thoughts, opinions, and preferences of the other and actively listened while the other spoke. Real talk is about exploring, discussing, listening, questioning, arguing, speculating, and sharing.[5] In real talk, people do not give up their ideas or ask others to give up their ideas; instead, people talk with one another and listen to one another about their ideas, hopes, and dreams. In real talk people do not hold forth, but rather discuss things with one another.

Neither Craig nor Jean assumed that each already knew the best ways to approach the committee assignments. Rather, they were hoping to learn about each other's preferences for committee leadership through their conversation. Through their dialogue, they were seeking connectedness with one another and the creative synthesis of their voices.

Dialogue is valuable because it helps us listen to others, share ideas with others, and make decisions with others. Dialogue also helps us discover a greater number of solutions for any given problem. In staff relationships, dialogue relieves men from the burden of expertise and frees women from the yoke of self-negation. As Craig and Jean are discovering, dialogue allows for the continued growth of the relationship and those in it.

The responses of people to these methods of communicating can be represented by a continuum.[6] On one extreme, some always like to be told what to do or to tell others what to do. On the other extreme, some seek constant dialogue. It is helpful for staff members to reflect on their preferred method of communication, talk about their preferences, and discuss how these preferences will influence their staff relationships.

Communication and Self Identity

Robert Nodding and Carole Dale, rector and associate rector at Trinity Episcopal Church, find that many factors affect their sense of self and their identity. Such factors include their past and current experiences, the roles they played and are playing in their personal and professional lives, and the feedback they receive from others. We develop an accurate and growing sense of our selves in our relationships with others. Because communication is the vehicle by which we relate with others, communication is crucial in developing a sense of self.

Studies indicate that people take men more seriously as speakers than they do women and do not hear women as well as they hear men. Women have more difficulty than men in asserting their authority or considering themselves as authorities, in expressing themselves in public so that others will listen, in gaining others' respect for their intellectual competence and their ideas, and in fully using their capabilities and training in their work. In their personal and professional lives, women often feel unheard even when they believe that they have something important to say.[7]

Effective communication embodies listening to others and others listening to us. When we do not listen, we do not attend to the voice or presence of others. We communicate most effectively when we value and respect others and want to hear their thoughts and feelings. Listening to others communicates care.

Many women feel that communication breakdown occurs because others are not interested in hearing them.[8] They feel "voice-less." This voicelessness may account for the greater prevalence of clinical depression and learned helplessness among women than among men.[9] Women often use the metaphor of voice when they talk about finding themselves. The development of a sense of voice, mind, and self are intricately intertwined.[10] For many women, being is intimately connected with being heard.

For many men, communication becomes difficult because they were raised to be strong rather than vulnerable. Vulnerability does not fit very well with expertise. Men socialized to be experts often develop a sense of self independent of others. Sometimes they can hear only their own voice. Many clergymen, however, do not seem to fit the stereotype of the strong, expert man. Clergymen often struggle with a feeling of voicelessness. Even if they have made a clear, conscious choice to relate to others as colleagues rather than as experts, this shift may intensify their sense of voicelessness. In addition, many clergymen and clergywomen feel voiceless because they serve an institution that has lost the authority that once was unquestioned.

As Robert and Carole talked together about how they communicated with each other, they found that these patterns fit with their experiences. Carole said that she felt most frustrated in their relationship when she sensed Robert was not listening to her.

She also told Robert, "I defer to you too much and hesitate to stand up for my beliefs, feelings, thoughts, and actions. I let your ideas and beliefs take precedence over mine."

Robert thought for a few minutes and then said: "Do I act as though I want you to give in to me?"

Carole, who was working at being more honest with Robert, surprised Robert and herself by saying: "Well, yes, I think you do. In subtle ways, you let me know your ideas are superior and sometimes you seem to blame me for things that don't go well. But that is my problem too."

Robert said: "Let me know when you hear me doing that."

Carole and Robert work toward communicating congruently, searching for words that correspond with their feelings. Such conversation may be confrontational, questioning, or supportive. As they communicate candidly, their self-esteem and their staff relationship may be enhanced.[11]

Carole was communicating congruently when she told Robert that she thought he acted as though his ideas were superior and that he sometimes seemed to blame her for things that did not go well. Carole and Robert were communicating congruently when they each took responsibility for their part of the problem.

Men and Women: Moving from Experts and Subordinates to Colleagues

Women and men have not only struggled with their roles, but also with how to communicate with one another out of those roles. Men were often raised to be strong, active experts and women were often raised to be passive, "nice" subordinates. Having experienced this different socialization, men and women are now seeking to learn how to be colleagues with one another. According to *The American Heritage Dictionary,* the word *colleague* comes from *com* which means "together" and *legare,* which means "choose"; thus, to be a colleague is to choose together.[12] As men and women explore choosing new roles for themselves and new ways of relating with one another, their preferred styles of communication can change.

Ray and Donna

Senior pastors like Ray can choose to be experts with their staffs or to be colleagues with their staffs. If Ray decided to learn how to be a colleague with Donna rather than always taking the role of expert, he would learn how to settle issues and make decisions in a collegial way with Donna. If Donna decided to work on being a colleague with Ray, she would talk directly with him about her feelings of hurt or anger when he talked "down" to her. Rather than withdrawing from Ray at these times, Donna would work toward facing Ray head-on and engaging him in conversation about her concerns. Collegiality between Ray and Donna would mean that they would talk with each other about their thoughts, feelings, and ideas while listening attentively to each other.

Craig and Jean

Craig and Jean relate to each other as colleagues. Although Craig remembers a time in his not-so-distant past when he needed to be an expert and be better than everybody else, he now strives to work with people of both sexes as equals. Craig's new identity in his staff relationship fits with Mark Gerzon's description of the colleague in *A Choice of Heroes.* Craig's identity as an expert was contingent on knowing more than everybody else, but his identity as a colleague thrives on cooperative, egalitarian staff relationships. As a colleague, Craig seeks to be a friend or mentor rather than the most insightful and brilliant member of the staff. He still respects expertise, but knows that it must be shared and enriched with the contributions of others in order to grow, and in order to invite cooperation. He wants to perform functions and tasks in an outstanding way, but does not want to dominate others. He prizes knowledge when it is used for enlightenment, but not when it is used to mystify people.

In the past, Jean's tendency as a "nice woman" was to listen to a lot of people, but not to talk much about herself. Now she is talking about her needs as well as listening to others speak of their needs. She has come to believe in herself and to love herself, as well as to believe in others and to love others. She has come to trust herself, as well as to trust others. Rather than unthinkingly relating as a subordinate with men perceived as experts, Jean realizes that she is an equal with men and that she can relate as a full partner with men. She also recognizes that while she is not an equal with the senior pastor, she is a valued member of the staff and needs to be honest about her thoughts, ideas, and feelings with Craig.

As women and men reflect on who they are and how they communicate with one another, they have an opportunity to develop a deeper awareness of who they are as women and men, and who they are in a mutual relationship with one another.

Communication and Power

Communication, in all of its forms, is an expression of power.[13]
Powerful people express their power in ways that are both covert
and overt. They show their strength by communicating either as experts—imparting knowledge—or as participants, speaking and
listening in turn. Powerful people are often confident in expressing
their own ideas and opinions—and confident enough to welcome
challenge and new insights from others.

Powerless people tend to communicate indirectly through the
use of derisive humor and sarcasm or passive body language and
angry silence. Some powerless people communicate their
insecurities either by claiming the role of expert or by giving up
their voice and waiting to be told what to do.

If we perceive power as a limited commodity and if we see
knowledge as a commodity of power, we will assume the expert
role whenever we can. If we perceive power as unlimited in supply,
we may find communicating through dialogue less threatening and
conclude that sharing ideas with others and listening to others'
ideas will empower everyone. In dialogue that includes everybody,
as one gains power, all gain power. When there is genuine dialogue,
there are no powerless people.

Most men and some women have been socialized to use the
expert model of communication, while some men and most women
have been socialized to take on the dialogue model of
communication. Once men and women are clearer about how they
communicate, they can make new choices about how they would
like to communicate in their staff relationships—as experts
imparting knowledge or as colleagues arriving at knowledge
together. AMN

Questions for Reflection and Discussion

1. *In your communication, do you tend to impart knowledge
   to others or arrive at knowledge with others?*
2. *If you are an "expert," what do you get out of your style of
   communication?*
3. *If you engage in dialogue, what benefits do you receive from
   communicating in this way?*
4. *If you want to engage in dialogue more and impart
   information less, how might you begin to change your style
   of communicating?*

5. *How does dialogue happen when one team member is new and the other team member has greater knowledge and experience?*

6. *What can you do if you are in a dissatisfying staff relationship and your colleague is satisfied with her or his role?*

NOTES

1. Mark Gerzon, *A Choice of Heroes: The Changing Face of American Manhood* (Boston: Houghton Mifflin, 1982).

2. Ibid.

3. Ibid.

4. Mary Field Belenky et al., *Women's Ways of Knowing* (New York: Basic Books, 1986).

5. Ibid.

6. Ibid.

7. Ibid.

8. Ibid.

9. Ibid.

10. Ibid.

11. Ibid.

12. Gerzon, op. cit., p. 251.

13. Ibid. Communication, in all its forms, is an expression of power.

CHAPTER VI

Work

Work Styles

Though religious leaders are called to center their energies on the re-ligious task (literally, "binding it all back together"), this task may hold different promises and costs for women and men in ministry. Men grew up with the message that they ought to focus their efforts toward a primary life challenge—a Dream, a Quest, a Calling. While concentrating on the "one thing most needful" brings the satisfaction of mobilizing one's energies toward one important end, this concentration can also yield a sense of impoverishment in the other, neglected spheres of life.

The focused lifestyle expected of men in the culture at large is mandated for those who have undertaken to be about the Lord's work and to respond to a sea of human need. The clergyman who has tried to give of himself emotionally all day may return home feeling so depleted that he does not have anything left to give to his wife and children. The pastor who urges others to volunteer some of their time in church and community may find he has no time to do so himself.

The more diffuse approach that often characterizes a woman's way of being in the world may incline her to notice the rich and varied connections in the whole picture that spreads out around her; yet that awareness may leave her feeling terribly stretched. How can she hold together all the elements of her complex, crowded life? Clergywoman Bailey Whitbeck finds it difficult even with a part-time job: "As I balance time at home, time at church, and time for myself, it does not add up to a total of one. There is that about the concept of 'part-time' which implies limit-setting. But *all* the areas of responsibility in my life tend to push beyond their limits. The expectations of husband, children, parents, and church is

that each of them is first in importance . . .and the half-time and
limit-setting go with those other responsibilities. . . . "[1] Women at the
most recent Alban Institute training event for male-female staff
teams reflected on the meaning of this collision between their
needs for a rounded life and the limitless human demands in the
congregation:

"There's a lot more than 'the minister' in me."

"I think it's important to think about my work in a way that
allows me to take a day off. I'm glad the senior minister sets a
livable pattern."

"The church goes on whether you're there or not. When I am
intentional about making the church independent of me, I'm
empowering the laity so I don't *have* to be there all the time."

When we put these two sets of approaches, promises, and problems—a man's tendency toward a more focused workstyle and a woman's tendency toward a more diffuse one—together on the same
church staff, we often find them in painful opposition. Katherine's
efforts to attend to all the parts of her life and to hold them in
balance sometimes leave Paul feeling frustrated. As he confided to
another clergyman, sometimes he thinks Katherine is not pulling
her weight: "If I had a male colleague, he'd be at the church sixty
or seventy hours a week the way I always have been. Katherine
won't put in more than fifty."

The common disjuncture between male and female workstyles
often brings frustration to women as well. In the workplace, which
is shaped by male assumptions and to which women have eagerly
sought admission, "work" means "what you do in the outside workplace." If success is measured by a male, focused workstyle, women
can not succeed unless they work that way too. As newcomers to
formal positions in church leadership, women have limited power
to reshape the prevailing norms, and those norms often make it
difficult for them to clarify and claim their own values. Said
Katherine, "I don't want to work like a driven person, but it's hard
for me to say that right out. I'm glad I have to meet the school bus
at 3:30 in the afternoon because that gives me permission to leave
my work at the church. Can you imagine what Paul's reaction would
be if I said, 'I'm going to leave at three because I want to take a nap
and a bath before I come back for the church dance'?" It is not
surprising that single clergywomen feel pressure to adopt
workaholic styles while many who are wives and mothers feel
stretched and conflicted.

In spite of the difficulties, clergywomen today may have a
prophetic responsibility to uphold their viewpoint about work in
the congregation. Katherine had an affirming "aha" when Paul con-

fessed concern about what he saw to be his driven workstyle. Katherine said to Paul, "Mostly, I've tried to stay faithful to my conviction that we are called to a balanced life. But at some level, I've been wobbly inside. When I looked up at the light burning in your office night after night as I locked up after a meeting and headed toward the parking lot, a voice inside said, 'Maybe that *is* what a minister ought to do—work all the time the way Paul does.' Thank you for telling me your doubts about the way you work." They look back to this conversation as a marker event in their struggle to live faithfully as workers.

As women move into new work and leadership roles, pressures to imitate men come from many directions. Men have traditionally had a limited number of roles, and our culture has assumed that the competent professional ought to focus on work. It is becoming increasingly clear, however, that women and men have substantively different experiences with roles. Women have learned to assume many roles from the time they were little girls. Women have developed coping skills and personal styles that equip them to move with some flexibility and ease among their various roles.[2] They know well the challenge of incorporating many different activities into an integrated lifestyle, though they may doubt their ability to meet that challenge.

Instead of assuming that multiple roles are a special problem for women serving on church staffs, it might be helpful for women and men to consider whether acknowledging many roles might enhance their ministry and the whole pattern of their lives. At the same time, of course, women as well as men must not lose sight of the other side of this tension, our need to discern "the one thing most needful" and pursue it faithfully.

For many staff teams, the conflicts between workstyles are compounded by a variety of styles of marriages. On church staffs today may be found some of the most traditional attitudes toward marriage and some of the newest experiments. The spread of attitudes is wider when staff members are of different generations. Marriage contracts are not only varied but also in flux and therefore under stress. Different styles of marriage present different pressures. Many traditional marriages are being reshaped as clergy wives join other women in the work force. In newer kinds of marital contracts, both partners get to do everything—but how are they to sort all that out and make it manageable?

It may take some negotiating for church staffs to forge contracts that hold promise of getting the essential tasks done, staying faithful to different values about work, and avoiding a setup for resentment. Katherine and Paul will find it helpful to talk honestly with one

another about their workstyles. What place does work hold in the
total structure of their lives? If their attitudes toward work differ significantly, how can they agree on expectations that leave neither feeling
overburdened or resentful? What part does continuing education
and time spent in the community and the larger church play in the
total work picture of each staff member? What messages does the
church salary structure convey about expectations for work and the
perceived value of work? Does the senior pastor's salary indicate
that he is expected to work much longer hours than his colleagues?
Does the assistant minister's salary carry an assumption that she is
pursuing the "mommy track" and does not want increased
responsibilities? Have these assumptions been tested? These
questions may need to be worked through with appropriate
ministry committees in the church.

How do staff members' workstyles witness to the Gospel? Does
the way Paul and Katherine work serve as a faithful and healthy
model for the working men and women in their congregation? As
colleagues wrestle with questions like these, important strengths in
partnership and ministry may emerge, and each may gain new
clarity about how they are called to carry out the religious task in
their lives as persons and as pastors.

Success

The new era of male-female collaboration upon which we are
embarking brings new kinds of difficulties and opportunities for
church leaders as they seek to be successful in ministry. With new
access to opportunities in formal church leadership roles, women
are pouring into ministry. Many seminaries report that more than
half the students and a large percentage of the more able students
are women. Many of those women bring life experience from
homemaking and other careers to their new roles as professionals
in ministry.

Clergywomen commonly report, however, that after an initial
placement they encounter a stone wall in their search for a
subsequent post. One Episcopal clergywoman reported that she
wanted a promotion but felt it was impossible; as she put it, people
liked having a "mommy priest" but were not ready for "mommy" to
take over "daddy's" job. K. R. Mitchell asks, "To what extent is it the
case that the specific kinds of jobs women can get on multiple staffs
are little different from the kinds of jobs available to them before
ordination became possible? The change is greater than most
people think, but smaller than most women clergy hoped for."[3]

Though women experience tougher competition for the pool of job opportunities, a pool that is shrinking in many denominations, clergymen are not immune from the effects of a tight job market made tighter by the increasing presence of women.

We may find new possibilities in what sounds like a pair of adversarial postures if we take a harder look at the question, What *is* success in the church? There are two very different kinds of answers to this question. First, the church is not exempt from the tyranny of "the ladder" that pervades the culture. As one Episcopal priest reported, "Of the 400 clergy in my diocese, I could count on my two hands the men who are . . . not bound by the upward-mobility mindset so prevalent in the Episcopal ministry."[4] This mindset carries with it performance anxiety, competition, and loneliness. It may also encourage a proactive stance toward one's career in ministry and a rejection of the passive dependence on mother church that has made many clergy feel helpless about taking active management of their working years.

A second, quite different, picture of success in ministry is easier to acknowledge. According to this picture, ministry is seen as a calling and a dedication of one's energies in the kind of servant leadership modeled in the ministry of Jesus. Clergymen are thus caught in a peculiar conflict: while the culture proposes a ladder view of success for men, they serve in a community that upholds values of obedient response to the call of God and service by God's people. One of the crazy-making features of this conflict is that acknowledging it and dealing with it openly are not seen as acceptable in church systems.

The male-female staff team may afford a helpful place to thrash out these issues. It may be a safer place, for many male clergy report that they feel less competitive toward female than toward male colleagues. Since the male-female staff team works close to the functional realities of parish ministry, with some distance from the ladders of the church hierarchy, team members may forge out fresh and workable answers to their questions about the meaning of success in ministry. What might those answers look like? Here is one example. Clergymen have been more reluctant than clergywomen to content themselves with positions as assistants. That attitude may be shifting, however, as some exchange hierarchical notions of success with a more functional look at what works and what does not work for the organization and what is satisfying and unsatisfying for people on church staffs. B. G. C. Bayne says that some of the best and the brightest clergy no longer seem to have their eyes on high-profile bureaucratic positions, but are looking to "portfolio" jobs on larger church staffs. "In specified positions on a staff, one often does the work for which one's gifts are suited and one's energies aroused, rather than serving as a generalist with unceasing, unrealistic, and unattainable demands to juggle."[5]

In Chapter V we noted Mark Gerzon's fresh interpretation of success in his proposal of "the colleague" as a new "image of American manhood." In contrast to the lonely "expert," the colleague's knowledge is used not to mystify, but to enlighten, not as a jealously guarded credential, but a gift to be generously shared. The colleague "is open to learning from women precisely because they are different from him" and he does not ignore his relationships in favor of his career goals.[6]

Male-female staff teams may also discover creative ways of living in the tension between advancement and calling as they balance society's focus on product with attention to process. Too often our culture's way of living and working ignores what is happening to people—*how* we are living together while we are trying to make the bottom line come out on top. The church's acknowledged norms are congruent with traditional feminine notions of success. What Jean Baker Miller calls "the 'lesser task' of helping other human beings to develop"[7] has been seen as both the feminine task and the church's task. There are, of course, times when the church does reflect the cultural devaluation of nurture, for instance, when Christian education is viewed as inferior work to be carried out by women.

The male-female team may provide a useful setting in which to forge out more collaborative definitions of success. Most of us are products of schools in which success was won by individuals who competed successfully with other individuals for the tokens of academic achievement. Against the background of such individualistic models of success, it was not surprising to hear staff team members in a recent training event saying directly or indirectly: "I feel successful when others esteem me. (And I feel nervous when my colleague is esteemed.)" Perhaps more collegial educational methods could help us develop a picture of what it looks like when "*we* are successful." Many of the teams in the training event had no idea what success in ministry looked like to their colleague and had not spent time forging a mutual vision of success. Commonly held goals will provide us also with a picture of mutual success in ministry.

Female-male teams can be helpful to people in ministry in yet another way: they give us a setting in which we can offer one another support in our movement toward success in ministry. Clergymen have had access to mentors and to power networks in

church systems, but have often been reluctant to open themselves
to needed support from persons other than their wives. (For their
part, women married to clergy often find themselves in an awkward
position: their husbands come home for support, but the wives
have no safe place to unburden themselves or seek counsel.) While
women in ministry have a hard time finding mentors or getting in
on the "old boys' grapevine," they have been more ready to look
for help from women's groups, friends, and parishioners. Male
pastors, therefore, can offer their sisters in ministry an entree to the
sources of power that provide new opportunities for stretching
their wings; women can offer their brothers permission to
acknowledge their vulnerability and need for support.

A lone clergywoman in a group of thirty local pastors
acknowledged that she was looking for ways to become more
competent in premarital counseling. Many of the other pastors felt
the need for the same kind of help, but had hesitated to
acknowledge it. As a result of the clergywoman's confession of her
own need, the ministers' group arranged for a course in premarital
counseling from which they all benefited. Another clergywoman
reported that she believed her male colleague's marriage had been
strengthened since they had been working as a team, because now
he could deal with parish worries at work instead of carrying them
home.

Male-female colleagueship in ministry can help all of us live in
the tension between power and vulnerability that accurately reflects
our ambiguous human situation. Acknowledgement of that tension
helps equip us for authentic ministry with others.

Serving as Models for Working Men and Women

Katherine and Paul are increasingly aware that the way they live
with their work speaks more loudly than the way they talk about
work in their sermons and classes; thus, they have tried to be
conscious of what they are modeling for the people of Christ
Church. Paul, particularly, is struggling to unlearn the lessons he
was taught as an intern under Pastor Hohle's supervision. Paul now
believes his supervisor inappropriately identified his work as pastor
with "the Lord's work" and therefore felt justified in neglecting his
wife and children and taking little notice of his parishioners'
ministries in the world. Katherine, as well, is getting firmer in her
convictions about her style of ministry as she evaluates her intern
experience with a driven pastor who seemed to her to contradict in
his behavior the gospel of grace he preached on Sunday mornings.

As they work to clarify alternative styles of working and ministering, Katherine and Paul are finding ways to live out some of their convictions: that all people (including clergy) are finite; that they themselves do not want to work as though work were their lord; that they want to move through their working day acting like cared-for people; that they intend to set boundaries to their work time and not allow all the spaces to get filled up by the press of duties; that they will not encourage a workaholic lifestyle in the church system—one that keeps people frantically busy with committees and meetings—but will be intentional about monitoring parish activity and "laying committees down," as the Quakers say, when their work is done. Both Katherine and Paul are trying to convey in their style of ministry their conviction that ordained ministry is no more holy than the ministry of lay people, and to create opportunities to hold up the ministries of lay people at home, in the workplace, and in the community.

In their conversations about work and prayer, the team has become aware of a paradox: while they encourage laity to discover the interconnectedness of prayer and work, they themselves must try to keep some separation between work and prayer. "It's too easy," said Paul, "to kid myself that I'm paying attention to maintaining my spiritual life when I'm planning for the prayer group or studying the Bible as part of my sermon preparation." Katherine and Paul have a contract to hold one another accountable for attending to the maintenance of their spiritual lives and for modeling faithful ways of working for the other Christians at Christ Church. CAH

Questions for Reflection and Discussion

1. *What place does work hold in the total structure of your life? Is that place different for you and your colleague? If there are differences, how can you honor them while you forge out equitable, mutual agreements about your responsibilities?*

2. *As you and your colleague(s) live them out in daily experience, how do your pictures of success in ministry coincide or contrast? In what ways might your parishioners benefit from the pictures of success you present—individually or jointly?*

3. *Have you articulated a shared vision for your ministry together? If not, what would be some first steps for doing so?*

4. *Are there ways you would like to ask your colleague to support you more helpfully?*

5. *As workers, what do you model for the people of your congregation? Does the culture of your congregation place a higher value on product or process, that is, the way you live together as distinguished from what you accomplish? How do you feel about the balance between product and process? If you think that balance needs shifting, what might be some specific ways to bring about that shift?*

NOTES

1. Bailey O. Whitbeck, "Clergy Struggle with the Pressures of Time," *Action Information,* Vol. XI No. 5 (September/October 1985).

2. Brunetta R. Wolfman, *Women and Their Many Roles* (Wellesley, MA: Wellesley College, 1985).

3. K. R. Mitchell, *Multiple Staff Ministries,* 142. (See Chap. IV notes.)

4. *New York Times,* 1 September 1985.

5. B.G.C. Bayne, "They Changed the Rules," *Action Information,* Vol. XIV No. 3 (May/June 1988).

6. Mark Gerzon, *A Choice of Heroes,* 254. (See Chap. III notes.)

7. Jean Baker Miller, *Toward a New Psychology of Women* (Boston: Beacon Press, 1976), 40.

CHAPTER VII

Attraction

Louis McBurney, an evangelical Christian and psychiatrist whose work has impressed me, says he can avoid falling in love with people other than his wife. I do not know what his secret is, but I do know that I am not in on it. Life certainly is simpler when I do not fall in love with my colleagues (and I usually do not), but it is exciting and challenging, as well as troublesome and painful, when I do. Here are some of my reflections on these experiences.*

When I find myself attracted to someone in a working relationship, my most elementary task, as I see it, may seem paradoxical: to be honest about the reality of my own experience and to behave responsibly.

First, I need to know what is going on inside me before I can make any choices at all. If I do not own my own feelings, I may pretend they belong to somebody else. I have heard more than one clergywoman say that when the senior minister was not able to recognize his attraction to her, she became the enemy. People who deny the human realities of their own lives behave in joyless and punishing ways toward the rest of the human community, as well as toward themselves.

It is not easy to acknowledge feelings of attraction toward people you are not "supposed" to be attracted to, and it is probably harder inside church settings than outside them. People do not talk about falling in love unless they are in the courtship stage of life. This silence accentuates their feeling of wandering alone, confused and uneasy in body, mind, and conscience. By removing the taboo

---

*I have found practically no wisdom in print on the subject of attraction between colleagues in ministry. I have therefore had to rely heavily on reflections about my own experience and the helpful comments of colleagues, consultants, and participants in learning events for male-female staff teams. CAH

against acknowledging these common human experiences, we may be able to help not only ourselves but also others to move through them more faithfully.

Second, I need to resist the temptation to act out my feelings inappropriately. I need to be faithful to my commitments to others and to my calling. As I see it, sexual activity belongs in marriage. As Jeremy Taylor points out, one of the purposes of sexual activity is to "endear each other" amid the duties, trivia, hardships, and boredom that are inescapable components of the dailiness of married life. If making love is the highest form of marital "team building," then it should be used to build that team. I need to be faithful to my calling as well: inappropriate sexual behavior destroys the authenticity of ministry as well as marriage.

Standing in this basic tension between awareness of my own feelings and responsible behavior is not easy. But the willingness to bear the discomfort of looking honestly at the reality of my own experience and refusing to act inappropriately on my feelings may, paradoxically, bring me a structure of reasonable comfort within which I can receive some gifts from this experience that comes so unbidden.

This basic tension is only the beginning. Once I have made the decision not to cop out in either of these basic ways, I encounter many more issues to wrestle with.

There are issues that have to do with my own growth. At a conference on women and men on the faith journey, my world was expanded by a Catholic priest who confessed, in a small group of embarrassed Methodist ministers, that he had found falling in love an occasion of spiritual growth. Perhaps he in his celibate life and I in a committed marriage each found that because we had rejected acting on such feelings, they could invite us to become curious about them. Released from the realm of *doing,* this great mysterious bundle of emotional energy can beckon us to explore more internal realities in the realm of *being.* Instead of faithless behavior or fruitless resistance (giving myself lectures: "Unrealistic!" "Immoral!"), I might ask: What is it that is trying to speak to me through the experience of having my attention inescapably drawn to this other person? Perhaps, by faithfully living with that question, I will tease apart the person and the projection. Projection can hold the promise of personal growth. In my experience, projecting on another person qualities I value can be a sort of halfway house toward a new stage of owning all I can be. I find that the power I thought belonged to another person is a power I can own for myself. I can remind myself that it was *my* energy that created that glowing center in my consciousness. So as I withdraw the projection, I have not lost anything; I have just waked up from a dream that it was *about somebody else.*

The level of my self-esteem makes a difference in my ability to handle feelings of attraction: I have discovered that these experiences of attraction I never asked for will be a lot easier for me to deal with if I have grown to the point where my self-esteem does not depend on the other's responding to me with the same intensity of feelings. Such feelings are idiosyncratic, and I will be steadier if my sense of being a worthwhile person does not depend on such evanescent stuff.

Attraction in working relationships raises important ethical issues too. We have already touched on one of them. I want to uphold the goodness of my nature as a sexual being. Those feelings are human and good. I agree with Shug Avery in *The Color Purple:* "God love all them feelings. That's some of the best stuff God did. . . ."[1] At the same time I want to be faithful to my commitments, putting them in an appropriately central place in my life. When I am caught between an event that seems to *happen* to me and my need to be responsible, struggle is an inescapable component. Church consultant Roy Pneuman points to a distinction that may be of some help in that struggle. The desire to celebrate an intimate relationship is part of our human nature. But we can choose whether public or private celebration is more appropriate to the nature and circumstances of a relationship. In organizational life the choice for private celebration often represents a failure, especially when it takes the form of acting out rather than talking out. Instead we can choose public ways of expressing our admiration for the one who is special to us—perhaps a book-autographing party or the presentation of a gift honoring an ordination anniversary.[2]

Another ethical issue lies in *letting the other have his or her own reality,* just as I want to own my own reality for myself. Male sexuality, as I read and hear about it, is more focused, more unambiguously and urgently genital. Men are more likely to sexualize a variety of experiences. Men have more fear, therefore, of losing control. If a man is avoiding standing in the primary tension, refusing to acknowledge his own feelings, he is likely to blame a woman if he becomes attracted to her.

Because the church has, in the main, used male experience as the norm in addressing sexual issues, it has viewed control issues as central. They are important. But they do not seem primary for most women. In one Alban Institute conference for male-female staff teams, the goals for the learning event clustered around the problem of dealing with attraction to female colleagues, while women's learning goals were varied, and there was no discernable "big issue." In another such training event, clergymen spoke about their discomfort with expressing affection toward their female colleagues:

"How can caring be communicated without sexuality issues becoming a problem?"

"One area that makes me uncomfortable is the display of affection. This is definitely gender-related. There are times when I'd like to hug her. A great deal of the hesitation has to do with the fear it might be misunderstood by church members."

Presbyterian minister Harry Winsheimer conducted an informal study of male-female teams that revealed a similar nervousness on the part of clergymen but not their women associates. Some of his male interviewees said they had adopted "deliberate behavior patterns" such as not going out to lunch with a female colleague. Winsheimer reported that "most of the women reacted with surprise when the question of sexual attraction and/or anxiety was raised."[3] The church, as I see it, has been one-sided in its preoccupation with rules, fear of loss of control, and projection of that loss of control onto women. We will achieve greater balance if we use not only men's experiences of attraction but women's too as we try to address this important area of human experience in the church.

According to what I read, and hear, and experience, women are more diffuse in their sexuality, more wholistic, more likely to see everything linked with everything else. They are more likely to globalize and spiritualize their feelings. A man is more likely to talk (especially with other men) about wanting to take a woman to bed, while a woman is more likely to talk about falling in love. As women respectfully acknowledge the more focused arousal of men, they might decide to moderate any inclinations they might have to engage in seductive behavior when seduction does not fit the situation. As we become more conscious of our own experience and more aware of how the experience of others differs, we will treat each other more caringly and respectfully.

Attraction opens up spiritual issues as well. The encounter of male and female does point to the image of God. The mystery of male and female, the energy and joy we may find in meeting another, point to our meeting with God, who is Other. Falling in love is one of the ways heaven tries to break into our hearts. Frederick Buechner tells how his first boyhood love pointed toward "all the beauty I longed for beyond the beauty I longed for in her."[4]

The encounter of male and female points to our longing for unity. I believe people who choose ministry as a profession have a strong wish for a unity of head and heart, body and spirit, which is promised by a radiant encounter with another. Those with iNtuitive Feeling temperaments, of whom there are a significant number in ministry, are powerfully led by this wish. Such encounters, with their attendant longings, are reminders that "thou hast put eternity in our hearts"—but not *answers* to those longings. Our culture's loss of a vision of the holy encourages people of our time to substitute love between men and women. Falling in love opens me up to yearnings that cannot be met by the one who occasions them. And so the yearnings are like a promise that cannot be kept. Meeting a new person who captures my attention is a little like looking at a blank sheet of paper. Anything could be written there, and there have as yet been no blots on the copybook. Herein lies an invitation to illusion. Life in all its beauty is hinted at in romantic love. So is loss and despair. But this recognition of the restlessness of my heart can be an opening. It may be a reminder that I need to "demythologize" my longings. What meets me as physical desire *may,* if translated and contained, be a crucible for my spiritual formation.

Because of their more diffuse sexuality, women can more easily sublimate sexual energy than men. Richard Olson says "men have gone after sex when they were really looking for something else— companionship, reassurance, self-esteem, intimacy."[5] The presence of this broader set of meanings under sexual guise may mean that *sometimes* men need to translate their sexual urges and fantasies. Even though it may be harder for men than women to take this energy and use it for spiritual purposes, it is obviously not impossible. Dante found his passion for God unlocked in just such energy, as did many men in the age of chivalry. Though our culture no longer suggests that this is possible, or even desirable, it may be a useful possibility to resurrect. Perhaps my Catholic priest acquaintance may have found that his vowed lifestyle made it easier for him to be clear that he was not going to express his attraction to a woman through sexual activity. Regarding ourselves as celibate in these relationships may press us to other meanings an experience holds. *Adelphoi*—brothers and sisters—may be a helpful word from our heritage for women and men in Protestant traditions.

The experience of falling in love raises issues about idolatry. Hildegard of Bingen cautions that if we are wise, we will know that God is in the center. When I lean too hard on someone who will not bear the weight of ultimate dependence, I find that the props always get knocked out from under me. I want to hold all gifts with an open hand, but there is something in me that wants to clutch them too. How do I hold lightly what strikes me like lightning? My feelings tell me to plant this preoccupation like a large tree in the center of my garden. My judgment tells me that in the total economy of my life this really is more appropriately a small flower to brighten the border. Obsessing carries with it an unmindfulness of the *many* gifts that life brings me every day. The promise for me is that perhaps in the space between loving and letting go I may encounter God.

Prayer has been essential for me in the midst of such emotional turmoils. As one fellow struggler has pointed out, while prayer can be a sneaky way to just keep on obsessing, it can also be the way to know that God is in the center, loving us passionately, and to consecrate our energies toward ministry.

Finally, attraction raises ministry issues. Energy for the work through graced partnership in ministry is surely one of the gifts of God for the people of God. As a gift it is not something to clutch, crave, or own, though it may take great effort to hold that gift with an open hand. Banked emotional fires can warm the tasks of ministry on church staffs and in clergy-lay partnership. Looking back to earlier centuries, we can appreciate the gifts the church has received from relationships in which spiritual intimacy fueled energetic outreach, like the relationship between Francis and Clare. Legend has it that the citizens of Assisi and Bettona saw what appeared to be a forest fire. "They ran to the scene prepared to combat a terrible blaze. But when they got to [the place where Clare and Francis were meeting] they could find no fire. All they saw was St. Francis and St. Clare and their friends sitting around a meager table, contemplating God. They understood that it had been a heavenly fire which they had seen and they left in awe and wonder."[6]

The giftedness of graced partnership in ministry is probably easier to come by at modest levels of attraction, where there is a gentle shimmer around the work, rather than consuming obsession. The combination of love and work is a potent one that packs a punch—for the enhancement or the crippling of ministry. A supervisor/subordinate relationship can add an additional layer of complex energy to the relationship, since the power of multiple roles makes for extra intensity and confusion.

As religious leaders, clergy or lay, we need to be crystal clear that authenticity is the foundation of our role. We need to live in a way that is consistent with the words and values about faithfulness we proclaim out of our tradition. People care deeply that their religious leaders be "for real" and find their behavior a travesty

when those leaders preside over the exchange of solemn vows and
then fail to keep their own commitments. Infidelity is deeply
destructive to the authenticity of ministry.

I write with feeling here because I once belonged to a church
whose pastor left his wife and children and headed off to the
tropics with a divorcee. As a lay person I found that this experience
deeply undercut my trust in the dependability of my religious
community and its leader. In our work at The Alban Institute, we
frequently learn of ministries wrecked in this fashion. The problem
has a deceptively low profile, however, because it seems cruel to
reveal specific instances of sexual misconduct as a factor in case
studies of involuntary terminations and other congregational
tragedies.

A pastoral counselor has recently written me that in the past year
she has encountered "what feels like an epidemic of clergy involved
in sexual relationships that have had disastrous effects on their
churches, their marriages, ministry in general, and themselves." She
writes, "I'm feeling quite overwhelmed at the pain that these
episodes have caused and the residue of lack of trust that will
linger in the churches for years. The 'goldfish bowl' of the local
parish means that there are issues of appropriateness that go
beyond whether someone is having an affair. Church staff members
need to get clear about what is too risky even if it doesn't seem
inappropriate at a personal level. In one of the cases we have been
involved with, a clergyman and a woman colleague have 'fallen in
love.' Both are married. They are spending more and more time
with each other (under the guise of work), and they are sharing
intimate feelings with each other that they do not share with their
spouses. The clergyman's wife (who already had very limited time
with her too-busy husband) is getting supplanted at an emotional
level, and this is as destructive to their marriage relationship as the
physical act would be. Perhaps there is infidelity without sexual
activity."

Colleagues who become absorbed in their attraction to one
another also run the risk of cutting themselves off from those to
whom they are called to minister. I remember one young
clergywoman who was in love with her male colleague and how
clear it was that she was only going through the motions in relating
to her parishioners. Her heart was otherwise engaged.

A final caution—colleagues in ministry who experience such
energy crackling between them will obviously do well to avoid the
temptation to process their feelings endlessly with one another.
When feelings are intense, a few sessions with a pastoral counselor

may help sort them out, provide support for living in the tension, and clarify the imperative for faithful behavior.

I have suggested here not ways to be sure you are "right" when attraction sparks between you and a partner in ministry, but rather some issues to consider with candor. In my experience, endeavoring to stand in the tension between honesty about my own reality and responsible behavior, paying attention to all the contradictions which I find in myself, trying to remain steady, and noticing when I am "off the rails" can lead to personal growth, spiritual opening, authenticity in ministry, and more sensitive companionship to others in the struggles of the heart. CAH

Questions for Reflection and Discussion

1. *If Kimberly or John came to you to confide that they found themselves attracted to their colleague in ministry, what counsel would you offer them?*

2. *What are the convictions from which you would derive such advice? How would those convictions find expression in your ministry to the women and men of your congregation?*

NOTES

1. Alice Walker, *The Color Purple* (San Diego: Harcourt Brace Jovanovich, 1982), p. 168.

2. Pneuman reports that this public/private celebration theory was drawn from a training model by Newt Fink and Cecil Benoit.

3. Harry Winsheimer, "Promises and Problems in the Teamwork of Male-Female Clergy Staffs," *Action Information* (Washington, DC: The Alban Institute, Mar./Apr. 1983).

4. Frederick Buechner, *The Sacred Journey* (New York: Harper & Row, 1982), p. 65.

5. Richard P. Olson, *Changing Male Roles in Today's World* (Valley Forge, PA: Judson Press, 1982), p. 55.

6. Bernard Bangley, *Spiritual Treasure* (Mahwah, NJ: Paulist Press, 1985), pp. 52–53. Reprinted with permission.

CHAPTER VIII

Women and Men as Partners in Ministry: Celebration and Challenge

Celebration seems to us the most important last word to emphasize in our discussion of the male-female staff team. Perhaps more than anything else, we need to pause and take time to appreciate the richness our partnership brings to our ministry—a rich colleagueship for us as ministers, a richer religious and theological perspective, broader understandings of leadership, and the possibilities of ministry with a wider range of people in the congregation. Of course, we face challenges as well. But let us stop first and look at all that is given. Many of us who choose a lifetime of ministry are the kind of superresponsible people Edwin H. Friedman calls "overfunctioners." We may have a tendency to skip over the gifts and move with tunnel-visioned concentration toward the next problem "we ought to fix." So let us pause first and move into the grateful, receptive mode that in itself may be one of the blessings of the female-male staff team.

What do we have to celebrate?

First, we can have a richer ministry together as colleagues than we could have as solo pastors or as same-sex teams. It is worth remembering that Jesus sent the disciples out two by two, that partnership in ministry figures importantly in the Pauline epistles, and that celibate couples brought new energy into missionary efforts in the next stage of the church's life. Energy is always heightened when differences are held together in tension; ministry embraces more dimensions when masculine and feminine strengths are brought together. As we join our gifts and perceptions as men and women, we may find that we discover a more whole picture of what success means, a picture that might be a prophetic offering to our society. We may find that we are better able to balance our focus on specific accomplishments with an attention to process—to *how* we are doing here in this church, as well as *what* we are doing. We may find ways to care about both competence and collegiality. In our most recent training session for male-female staff teams, one senior minister was clearly celebrating both when he said of his associate, "She has come forward with better ways of doing things, and I have been open to implementing them in the life of the church." This head-of-staff was in touch with the broader vision that can encourage us to join both assertiveness and compassion in our work together, and to model an easier way of shifting between them to the people with whom we minister. We may be able to offer and receive support in a way that we did not know as solo ministers.

Our partnership in ministry may bring us some of the joys of intimacy on the job. Speed Leas has spoken helpfully of the kind of intimacy that can develop on staff teams.[1] This intimacy includes *vulnerability*. In a relationship that allows me to be vulnerable, I can share my fears and hopes—things I feel tender about. I can acknowledge my dependence on you, and give up some of my need to control. Intimacy includes *commitment*. Though this commitment may not be long-term, it means that I care about you. Our relationship matters to me. I will stick with you, even if you do wrong. I am on your side in spite of what you did—even to me. Intimacy includes *bonding* and *identifying*. We have a sense of "we." When you are upset, I get tense. I have a sense of being involved in what you do: when you make a mistake, I have the feeling *I* did it.

Second, as women and men joining our strengths on the church staff, we are building toward greater wholeness in our religious and theological perspectives. Our perceptions of the faith incorporate but transcend the traditional "generic" assumptions, which are often based on male experience alone, and may now include more fully the experience of both men and women. Together we forge a more inclusive view of the human situation: for example, we learn to include not only pride but hiding in our understandings of how people miss the mark. We gain a broader repertoire of approaches to ethical decisions: to our concerns about principles, fairness, and rules, we join a commitment to relationships and to the ties that bind a community together. We may become more concerned about the *humanity* of Jesus than about the *maleness* of Jesus. Our joining of men and women on the staff team may quietly raise the profile of enfleshment—surely a central part of our creed and our experience, but often ignored in the average church's day-to-day working theology. As we become more aware of our enfleshed nature, we may find that issues related to sexuality become more accessible, more readily dealt with in our ministry with the men and women in our congregation. And our experiences as men and women may meet to open up a broader range of ways to describe God and to speak of One who includes and transcends what we know of human personhood, both male and female. We discover approaches to our spiritual journey we had never before envisioned, and hitherto hidden perceptions of our faith emerge. We may be warmed by the erotic dimensions of our relationship with the Lover of Souls.

Third, our ministry may be enriched not only as colleagues and as theologians, but also as *leaders*. Here, too, we experience that "it is not good for the man to be alone." Our team gives a powerful message that ministry happens in relationship. Our *partnership* carries compelling messages. In contrast to the expectation set up by solo leadership that "he will have it all for us," we open up ministry for others and invite them to join us as we pass leadership responsibility back and forth. As each of us shifts between proactive and receptive modes, we allow space for others to take initiative as well, thus saying in effect to laity, "You come minister too."

As we join leadership styles that may be different, we may gain new comfort with standing apart or alongside, and new flexibility in shifting from one posture to another as the needs for leadership change. And so we may point more faithfully to both the transcendence and the immanence of the Holy One. Understanding that vulnerable leaders lead us all into religious power, we may support one another in claiming both our power and our vulnerability. We can thus become leaders to whom others can more easily open the hurting places in their lives, and leaders who invite others to claim their power and authority just as we claim our own. In both these ways, we empower laity for ministry.

Fourth, as a male-female team, we can minister effectively with a broader range of our parishioners than could a single pastor or a single-sex team. Neither elderly men who love the tradition of their church nor abused women will retreat to the edges of the community because they feel their pastor can not understand what is important to them. Together, we can be important models for *all* the people. Our "working partnership" will serve as "a microcosm of the church," says K. R. Mitchell. Since God works through a *people*, "ministry in multiple forms, through teams or staffs, is a reflection of the church and thus a reflection of God's preferred way of working with us."[2]

As we struggle to make our partnership more effective, the struggles of all women and men will become more visible. Our parishioners will sometimes tell us how important we are to them as symbols of partnership—how powerful it is for them to see us celebrating the Eucharist together, to hear preaching in different voices, to hear different accents in church management and pastoral care. These everyday parish events speak more powerfully than many words or many pages of denominational resolutions about the full participation of women and men in ministry. We can carry this symbolism consistently through our ministry with the people of our congregation by using our teamwork as a teaching tool, and by recruiting male-female teams as teachers and co-chairs of committees.

Of course our work together in female-male teams is an occasion not only for celebration but also for challenge. Only you are in a position to discern what particular challenges need to engage the attention of your own team, but we can review some possibilities for your consideration.

Many of us in male-female staff teams need to be alert to issues of self-esteem—our own and that of our colleagues. We need to notice ways in which our self-esteem issues are gender-related, and to work with those issues openly as a team so that we may enhance our ministry, as both individual and partner. We may find that we are challenged to stretch our sense of our own self-esteem and our ability to support that of others. This seemed to be happening for one INTJ senior minister, an independent innovator, whose new ENFP assistant minister is a brilliantly empathic "people person." He said, "I feel a twinge of jealousy when other people praise Sally as warm, in touch with her feelings."

Communication may be a challenge for us. We need to learn to listen, to speak, to hear and be heard in different voices and with attentive ears. We may need to break through some ancient and unhelpful assumptions we have about men and women that lead us into patterns of blaming or placating.

Our different approaches may open up areas of conflict between us. As we address them, we may be sending useful messages to the parish about the inevitability and the manageability of conflict.

Out of our diffuse or focused workstyles, we may find ourselves challenged to negotiate a way of working together. Yet our struggle toward some commonly held approaches to our work may in itself be an offering to the people of our parish, as we all open up these difficulties in partnership which everybody faces and discover new perceptions and new solutions.

And there may be challenges that arise out of our close relationship as partners in ministry. Though intimacy is full of promise, it proposes problems as well. Speed Leas has pointed out that one of the characteristics of intimacy is that it excludes others. If we have a special relationship, then others do not participate in it. If we are set apart in our partnership, others may feel like outsiders. The role of the pastor's wife, the parish secretary, and long-term parish leaders may shift in some ways. The staff team will need to find ways of holding their own gift of close colleagueship with a hospitable openness. Some members of teams will encounter challenges arising from their attraction to one another. They will need to struggle for personal awareness and hold to responsible behavior, to channel the helpful energy that arises from this partnership in ministry. They may need to pray for the grace to hold their encounter as an icon, one of those spaces where the holy shines through, rather than as an idol, which blocks that space.

Some of those challenges will be the other side of the richness you celebrate in your partnership. CAH

Questions for Reflection and Discussion

1. *What are you grateful for in this partnership in ministry? Ponder this question carefully in preparation for your meeting, perhaps writing out your answers and giving each other a copy. Go over your reflections together. Where you need clarification or an example, ask for it.*
2. *What two or three challenges invite your attention? Decide on your own answer to this question in preparation for your session. Then take time together to clarify and agree on your answers. What are some first steps for addressing each? Make an appointment for three to four weeks from now to review progress on the first steps and determine subsequent steps.*

NOTES
   1. Lecture at Male-Female Staff Teams Conferences.
   2. K. R. Mitchell, *Multiple Staff Ministries,* 28. (See Chap. IV Notes.)